"The universe is full of magical things patiently waiting for our wits to grow sharper."

Eden Phillpotts

Why Haven't We Seen Aliens?
by Stephen Rickard

Published by Raven Books
An imprint of Ransom Publishing Ltd.
Unit 7, Brocklands Farm, West Meon, Hampshire GU32 1JN, UK
www.ransom.co.uk

ISBN   978 178591 694 6
This hardback edition first published in 2019

Copyright © 2019 Ransom Publishing Ltd.
Text copyright © 2019 Stephen Rickard

Cover design by Stephen Rickard.

A CIP catalogue record of this book is available from the British Library.

All rights reserved. No part of this publication may be reproduced, stored in a retrieval system, or transmitted, in any form or by any means, electronic, mechanical, photocopying, recording or otherwise, without the prior permission of the publishers.

The right of Stephen Rickard to be identified as the author of this Work has been asserted by him in accordance with sections 77 and 78 of the Copyright, Design and Patents Act 1988.

WHY HAVEN'T WE SEEN ALIENS?

STEPHEN RICKARD

RAVEN

" The trouble with facts is that there are so many of them."

Samuel McChord Crothers

CONTENTS

1 Where are They?   **11**
    What are aliens?   11

2 Three Choices   **15**
    There aren't any aliens   15
    We've already met them   16
    We just haven't met them yet   29

3 A Quick Tour of the Universe   **31**
    Our solar system   31
    The building blocks of the universe   36
    Galaxies   40
    Galaxy groups and superclusters   45
    What's all this got to do with aliens?   47

4 The History of the Universe   **51**
    Where did the universe come from?   51
    Old ideas about the beginning   52
    A quiet revolution   54
    Light won't behave   66
    The expanding universe   73
    The Big Bang   76
    The COBE satellite   79
    Is the universe infinite?   82

" Twinkle twinkle little star
How I wonder what you are
Up above the sky so bright
Like a diamond in the night."

Ann Taylor and Jane Taylor

How big is the universe?	85
Our aliens	87

5 Life 91

What is life?	93
Evolution	95
Evolution is blind	103
Where does life come from?	107
How did life start?	109
Where did life start?	112
Is water essential for life?	114
The habitable zone	116
How quickly does life get going?	120
Timeline Earth	123
Intelligent life	126
What will aliens look like?	133

6 Wrong Place, Wrong Time 141

Wrong place?	144
Wrong time?	155
So that's why we haven't seen aliens	158
Looking back in time	160
Is time travel possible?	163
Wormholes	166

7 Looking for Aliens 169

SETI	169
False alarms	172

" The good thing about science is that it's true whether or not you believe in it."

Neil deGrasse Tyson

Voyager's Golden Records	178
Messages that wait	180
The Drake equation	181
How could we say 'Hello'?	186
Do we really want to meet aliens?	192
8 Have We Got It All Wrong?	**197**
(Further thinking)	
Carbon versus silicon	198
Unexpected messages	202
Our science is wrong	208
Multiple universes	217
The Big Crunch	218
Glossary	**221**
Word List	**237**
Image Credits	**241**
About the Author	**247**

> The surest sign that intelligent life exists elsewhere in the universe is that it has never tried to contact us.

Calvin and Hobbes

WHERE ARE THEY?

This book asks a simple question. 'Why haven't we seen aliens?'

In other words, if aliens exist, then surely they would have visited us by now. They would have come to our planet Earth. So by now we should have seen them, met them, greeted them …

So why haven't we? Does it mean that aliens don't exist?

What are aliens?

What do we mean when we talk about 'aliens'?

If you've watched Star Wars, or E.T., or Star Trek … or any one of hundreds of other science-fiction films or TV programmes, or if you've read any science-fiction stories, you'll have a pretty good idea of what aliens are supposed to look like. Usually they are supposed to look a bit like us (sometimes a bit taller or a bit shorter) and sometimes they have funny things stuck on their heads, or they are odd colours, such as grey, or blue or green.

Your average, standard movie alien

Sometimes aliens are shown with five fingers – although sometimes they have four, or three. (The number of fingers they have might turn out to be very important, as we'll see later.) Sometimes we see them with tentacles instead of arms or legs.

It's strange, but aliens in movies began to look a lot more, well, *alien*, as movie make-up (and computer generated images, or **CGI**) got better. If you watch some old **science-fiction** movies from the 1950s (ask your parents or your grandparents!) you'll see that aliens in those days really just looked like actors in a rubber suit.

What we really mean when we talk about 'aliens' is creatures, or living things, that don't come from our own planet Earth. Actually that's pretty close to a **dictionary** definition: the Cambridge online dictionary says that alien means 'coming from a different country, race or group', or 'strange and not familiar' or 'relating to creatures from another planet'.

So, for our purposes, aliens are living creatures that have come here from another place in the **universe**.

Is that a good definition? Well, it's a start. Let's use it until it stops being useful for us.

> "It ain't what you don't know that counts, it's what you know that ain't so."

Will Rogers

THREE CHOICES

So, let's ask the question again. Why haven't we seen aliens? Well, we need to start somewhere, so let's start with three possible answers:

1. There aren't any aliens. This is why we haven't seen them.
2. There *are* aliens and we've already met them. They've already visited planet Earth.
3. There might be aliens and, if there are, then for whatever reason we just haven't met them yet.

There aren't any aliens

First answer: there aren't any aliens. That's why we haven't met them.

Just think about that for a moment. If this answer is correct, it means that in the whole wide universe – amongst *everything* that has ever existed or will ever exist – the only living things are those that we find on our own planet Earth: humans, ducks, sheep, daisies, bacteria and all the rest of it. So there is nothing living anywhere else in the universe: no other **planet**, **moon**, **star**, **asteroid** or anything else, anywhere else *anywhere*, has a living thing on it.

That seems to me to be quite a startling suggestion. Especially when we start to think about how big the universe actually is (something we'll do in the next chapter). It would mean that we are all alone in the universe.

Of course, it might be true: we might be all alone. If that is the case, then we have the answer to the title of this book. But how can we prove it? How can we prove that we are all alone? As we'll see later, I don't actually think we can. Not yet anyway, and probably not for a long time – if ever.

So let's leave this answer for the moment. Let's take a closer look at the universe around us over the next few chapters, and then we can look again at the possibility that there is no life anywhere else in the universe.

We've already met them

Second answer to the question 'Why haven't we seen aliens?': perhaps aliens have actually visited us already, and we have seen them – or at least we've seen their **technology**.

Judging by reports in the media every now and then, it definitely seems to be true that we have already been visited by aliens. What we seem to see most often are UFOs – **Unidentified Flying Objects** – and they are usually in the shape of flying saucers or bright, flashing lights. Sometimes, the reports say, a UFO crash-lands on Earth and a few humans get to see the wreckage – and perhaps even a real-life, dead alien.

The most famous of all the reported events like this is supposed to have happened near a place called **Roswell** in **New Mexico** in **1947**. Some wreckage of a crash was discovered, and the story went around that it was a crashed alien flying saucer.

The Roswell Daily Record newspaper reports the 'captured flying saucer'. July 9th 1947

Hundreds of books have been written about this one crash, but in fact it looks very much as though the wreckage was of an American government weather balloon, rather than a UFO.

Even so, there have been many, many reportings of UFO sightings throughout history, going back thousands of years. Even the **ancient Egyptians** reported that they saw UFOs. Nearly three and a half thousand years ago, the scribes of **Pharaoh Thutmose III** were supposed to have written that 'fiery disks' were encountered floating over the skies.

A statue of Pharaoh Thutmose III

Of course a UFO is exactly that – an *unidentified flying object*. So anything moving in the sky that we can't identify is a UFO, whether it is a piece of wreckage from an aeroplane, a shooting star, aircraft lights at night or an alien spacecraft. Calling it a UFO just means that we haven't worked out what it is yet.

This isn't a book about searching for UFOs, so we're going to have to stay focused and move on. But it's worth remembering this: just because a UFO has been spotted, doesn't mean that it's an alien spacecraft. If we're looking at UFOs to work out whether aliens have visited us, what we really need is **conclusive proof** that something could only be alien – or part of an alien technology. So far we haven't seen this.

Of course the smarty-pants answer to the question, 'Why haven't we seen aliens?', is to say that aliens are already here. Smarty-pants answer version one says that aliens are regular visitors to planet Earth; smarty-pants answer version two says that aliens are actually living amongst us now, here on Earth.

If either of these answers were true, then why haven't we seen these aliens, if they're so common?

Well, I can think of at least three explanations.

- The aliens might be **invisible**. (Is that even possible?) But even if our aliens were invisible, wouldn't we bump into them in the street? And surely, even if they were invisible, wouldn't we still see some evidence of their daily activities: their homes, their technology (if they have any), the heat given off by their bodies (their **heat signatures**), even the rubbish they throw away. All living things affect the **environment** that they live in in some way, and we should be able to detect that.

  The famous scientist **James Lovelock** (he invented the **Gaia theory**, if you've heard of it) was once asked to think about how to look for alien life on other planets. Everybody else was trying to work out how to look at the surface of the planet, trying to 'see' aliens moving about. But Lovelock suggested a different way of

James Lovelock

doing it. Rather than looking for the aliens themselves, he suggested that we look for the effects alien life would have on the atmosphere, or the **biosphere**, of their planet. On Earth, animals change the atmosphere of our planet by breathing in **oxygen** and breathing out **carbon dioxide**; plants do the opposite. Both of these activities change the amounts of those two gases that make up the atmosphere. Living things change the atmosphere in other ways, too.

In other words, said Lovelock, don't look for life; look for the *effects* of life. That was a very clever solution to a difficult problem.

The aliens might be too small. I remember reading a fantastic story as a child about an alien invasion fleet on its way to destroy Earth. There were thousands of alien spaceships, each filled with thousands of alien soldiers, all primed and ready to attack and take over Earth. The alien fleet radioed Earth, demanding that everybody surrender, but the people on Earth couldn't see any alien fleet, even though they could receive the radio messages.

The story ended with the entire invasion fleet crashing into the eye of a person walking down the street in a small town in America. He just said, 'Hang on, I've got something in my eye,' and wiped it away, just as you wipe away a speck of dirt in your eye. Millions of aliens (and their spaceship fleet) were all smaller than a speck of dirt.

Could alien life forms be **microscopic** in size and still have very advanced technologies (certainly technologies far more advanced than ours) to reach our planet? Building spaceships smaller than a speck of dust would mean that they'd need to be experts in **nanotechnology** – building things by working with individual molecules and atoms.

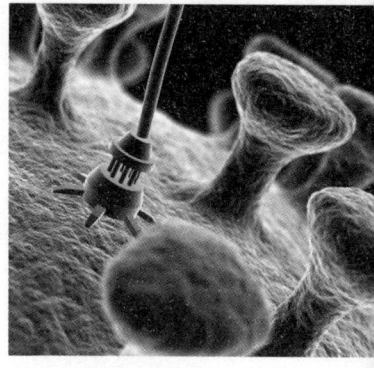

Nanotechnology

Here's another thought: what if it wasn't the aliens that were microscopic, but it was us. What if planet Earth and all life on Earth, including us, was microscopic in size compared to the aliens? Would we be able to see them then? Or would they just be too big to see?

A third reason why we might not be able to see these aliens that are supposedly all around us is that they might be hiding. Perhaps our aliens are living deep underground, or at the bottom of the sea.

This isn't as daft as it sounds. Even now there are many types of creatures living at the bottom of the sea that we have never seen and know nothing about. We know that, because we keep finding new, surprising creatures.

For example, in 1979 scientists discovered particular kinds of creatures living at the bottom of our oceans. These creatures live near **hydrothermal vents**, which are fissures, or cracks, in the sea floor, from which very hot water, heated by the interior of our planet, continually shoots out. Sometimes this water is very, very hot – up to 464 degrees **Celsius**: much hotter than the boiling point of water. (The water doesn't boil because of the huge pressures so far down.)

According to our understanding of life, the creatures living around these hydrothermal vents should not be able to survive – yet they're not only surviving, they're thriving. In fact whole communities of creatures have evolved to live in these places. The vents in the sea floor release minerals as well as hot water, and as a result dark chimneys of minerals form, called **black smokers**.

Black smokers – hydrothermal vents deep under the sea, teeming with life. East Scotia Ridge, Southern Atlantic Ocean

The creatures living around these black smokers made a very important contribution to our understanding of biology; they taught us that our thinking up to that point about what was necessary to create life was simply wrong. Life can exist (quite happily it seems) in places where we used to think that life was simply impossible.

Tubeworms living next to hydrothermal vents in the Galapagos Islands

This is really important when we start thinking about life elsewhere in the universe. In fact, these black smokers helped create a completely new science, called **astrobiology**.

Fifty years ago the search for life elsewhere in our solar system focused mainly on the planet **Mars**.

The surface of Mars ('Mount Sharp') – photographed in 2015 by NASA's Curiosity rover

Of all the planets in the Solar System, scientists thought, Mars is the one most like Earth. So it seemed the most likely place to find life beyond Earth.

It is still possible that there is life on Mars, but scientists are now looking much more closely at two small moons, far, far out in the darkness of space. The planets **Saturn** and **Jupiter** are huge, cold planets, too far from the Sun to receive anything like enough heat to support life.

But scientists are getting very excited about Jupiter's moon **Europa**, and Saturn's moon **Enceladus**. Why? Because it is very likely that both moons have active hydrothermal vents, just like the hydrothermal vents on Earth.

Saturn's moon Enceladus

The vents on these two moons (if vents do exist there) were created by the huge pressures on these moons, caused by the **gravity** of the massive planets they both orbit. Suddenly we are thinking that there might well be life on both of these moons.

Enceladus is particularly interesting: it is mostly covered by ice, with giant water (yes, water!) geysers spewing water and ice out into space.

Geysers on Saturn's moon Enceladus spewing water and ice out into space (photo taken by the Cassini space mission)

We also think that there is an ocean under the surface of Enceladus, and we have even detected heat escaping from the inside of the moon, showing that it is geologically active.

We are the aliens

Now here's a thought: what if aliens are already here on Earth ... and *we* are the aliens. Yes, us, the human race, are the aliens from another world. In fact, maybe all living things on Earth are aliens.

Is that a daft idea? Well, there is a theory that scientists call **panspermia** that says exactly that. The suggestion is that life (in the form of **microorganisms**) exists pretty much everywhere throughout the universe, and is spread by space dust, comets, asteroids and other stuff out there.

The theory suggests that microorganisms can survive in the cold of space (where it is very cold, usually very dark and there is no atmosphere) in a kind of hibernation. Then they 'come back to life' when they arrive at a suitable planet. At that point this life can grow, evolve and eventually become ... us!

We don't know yet if this is more than just a theory, but we do know that molecules containing **carbon** (we call them **organic molecules**) are found in space. That's important because, as far as we know, all life is based on carbon molecules. Organic molecules contain the building blocks of life and living things.

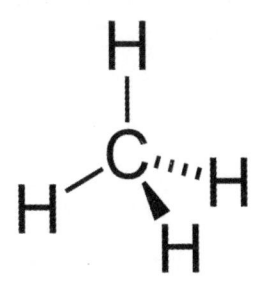

We know that organic molecules such as methane are found in space

If the theory of panspermia were true, then it's certainly possible that all life on Earth did originally come from space. It would also mean that there is likely to be life on other planets – as long as those planets have the right conditions for life. (We'll talk about that later on in Chapter Five.)

So could panspermia be true? Well, just think about this:

- We know that organic molecules can survive in empty space.

- The Nobel prize winning scientist **Francis Crick**, along with his colleague **Leslie Orgel**, has even suggested that life may have been purposely spread by an advanced **extraterrestrial** civilization. (So we are like seeds that some aliens planted on planet Earth – their little backyard garden.) Is he right? No idea.

- In 1960 **Thomas Gold**, Professor of Astronomy at Cornell University, went a step further. He suggested that life on Earth might be the result of what he called 'cosmic garbage'. A long time ago, he said, some extraterrestrial beings might have dumped some rubbish on Earth – and we evolved from that rubbish! (Just like when you throw an apple core out of the window, and eventually an apple tree grows from it.)

But of course, even if panspermia were true, it still doesn't answer the question: are we (meaning 'all life on Earth') alone?

We just haven't met them yet

We're still discussing the three possible answers to the question, 'Why haven't we seen aliens?'.

And here's the third (and final) possibility: maybe there is life elsewhere in the universe, but we just haven't met it yet. And they haven't met us.

Is that a possibility? Of course.

How would we go about proving it? Well, one thing we can't do is look in every corner on every planet in the universe, on the off-chance that we might find life (or signs of life). The universe is just too big, and there are way too many planets (and moons and other objects) for that to be a practical solution.

Rather, we need to look at the **probabilities** of life existing elsewhere. We need to ask ourselves, 'What are the chances?'

And answering that question means that we need to get a better understanding of how big the universe actually is, how old it is, how life begins, what is needed for life … and so on.

Answering *those* questions will take up most of the next four chapters of this book.

So let's start by looking at the universe itself.

"Science is a way of trying not to fool yourself."

Richard Feynman

3

A QUICK TOUR OF THE UNIVERSE

If we're going to think about the chances of our actually meeting aliens, we need to understand a bit more about this universe that we are part of.

Let's start with some basic facts, by describing the universe that we can see around us.

Our solar system

We live on a planet which we call **Earth**. This planet orbits a star which we call the **Sun**. Earth is the third planet from the Sun; **Mercury** is the closest planet, then **Venus**, Earth and five more planets: **Mars**, **Jupiter**, **Saturn**, **Uranus** and

Our Solar System

The Sun and the planets in our solar system, showing the relative sizes of each.

Mercury
4,800 km diameter

Venus
12,100 km diameter

Earth
12,700 km diameter

Mars
6,800 km diameter

Jupiter
140,000 km diameter

Saturn
120,500 km diameter

Uranus
51,000 km diameter

Neptune
50,000 km diameter

The Sun
1.39 million km diameter

Neptune, in that order. (Until 2006 **Pluto** was also defined as a planet and was always described as the ninth planet orbiting the Sun. But in 2006 it was demoted to 'dwarf planet', rather than being a planet in its own right.)

Our planet Earth has a **diameter** of about 12,700 km; the smallest planet, Mercury, has a diameter of about 4,800 km and the largest planet, Jupiter, has a diameter of about 140,000 km. These are all small compared to our star, the Sun, which has a diameter of about 1.39 million km. (Numbers are numbers; it's easy to miss just how small the smaller planets — including our own planet Earth — actually are. Perhaps the diagram opposite will help you appreciate these relative sizes. And look at Mars — for all the fuss we make about going there, it's not very big, is it?)

Taken together, the Sun, the eight planets and all the other objects in space that are affected by the Sun's gravity form what we call the Solar System.

Next, let's look at how far the eight planets are from the Sun. Mercury, the planet nearest the Sun, is very roughly 55 million km distant from the Sun.

It's not too difficult to imagine distances of say a few thousand kilometres — after all, that's just a long distance flight from say New York to London.

But in space we quickly find ourselves talking about distances that are very big numbers indeed — far too big really to understand. So when scientists talk about the Solar System, they often use the measurement **Astronomical Unit**, or **AU**. One AU is defined as the distance from the Earth to the Sun (which is about 150 million km). So instead of saying for example that the planet Neptune is 4.5 billion (4,500,000,000) km from the Sun, we just say that it is 30 AU distant from the Sun. So the distance from Neptune to the Sun is thirty times greater than the distance from the Earth to the Sun. That makes it a bit easier to understand.

The diagram opposite shows the Sun and the eight planets again, this time showing their **relative distances** from the Sun. The planets aren't shown to scale, but you can see straight away that the four smaller planets (Mercury, Venus, Earth and Mars) are all pretty close to the Sun (relatively speaking). After that, things start to get really spread out.

These distances can be quite hard to imagine. It's difficult to get a feel for how big our solar system really is – and the huge spaces in between (most of our solar system, most of the universe in fact, is empty space).

Another way of thinking about these distances is to convert them into time. Imagine I was travelling in a space-ship at the speed of (say) 25,000 km per hour. That's nearly 7 km per second.

How long would it take me to get to each planet, if I was travelling from the Sun?

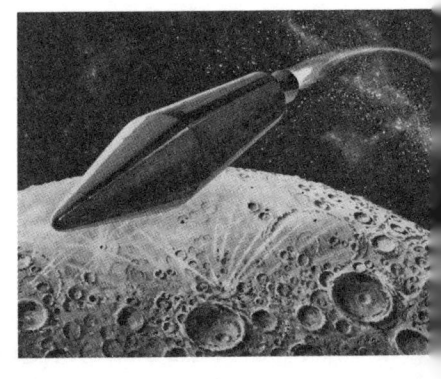

Distances of the planets from the Sun

The planets in our solar system, showing their relative distances from the Sun. The planets are not shown to scale.

The Sun

Mercury
0.4 AU

Mars
1.5 AU

Venus
0.7 AU

Earth
1.0 AU

Jupiter
5.2 AU

Saturn
9.5 AU

Uranus
19.2 AU

Neptune
30.1 AU

Visiting the planets from the Sun – at 25,000 km per hour	
To visit:	Would take:
Mercury	100 days
Venus	175 days
Earth	250 days
Mars	375 days
Jupiter	more than 3.5 years
Saturn	more than 6.5 years
Uranus	more than 13 years
Neptune	more than 20 years

So, to get this in perspective, a space rocket travelling at 25,000 km per hour would take more than 20 years to travel from the Sun to the planet Neptune. A **round trip** is going to take twice that – about half a lifetime! In case you haven't realised yet, our solar system is a big place. Getting around is a bit more time-consuming than a trip to the local shops.

The building blocks of the universe

Now let's move on, and ask ourselves how our solar system fits into the rest of the universe.

You may have noticed that so far I have referred to our solar system as 'the Solar System'. Capital S, capital S. That's because we call our solar system, 'The Solar System' (just as we call Earth's moon, 'The Moon'). But our solar system is not the only one in the universe. There are many more. Many, many, *many* more.

In fact, scientists think that it's quite likely that every single star in the universe is at the centre of a solar system. In other words, every star in the universe might have planets orbiting it, and some of those planets will probably have moons orbiting them.

Until about thirty years ago this was no more than a theory, but recent advances in building powerful telescopes and other sensitive data-collecting instruments mean that scientists can now actually 'see' planets orbiting far-away stars.

That's not quite true: they can't *see* the planets, because the planets are dark and very, very far away. What they *can* do is use a number of techniques to **infer**, or work out from the evidence, that a planet is there. For example, when a planet orbits a star, it passes in front of the star for part of its orbit. As a result, the

When a planet passes in front of its star, the amount of light we see given out, or emitted, by the star is reduced

amount of light that we see coming from that star dips ever so slightly as the planet passes in front of it. By measuring how much the light dips, and by recording how often it happens, scientists can calculate the size and orbit of the planet that's making the light dip.

Planets that orbit other stars are called **exoplanets**. Scientists have discovered, for example, that the star they call **Kepler 11** has six exoplanets orbiting it. Of course there may be more planets than that; it's just that we've detected six so far.

An artist's impression of six exoplanets orbiting the star Kepler 11

(It's worth pointing out that, with our current technology, it's the larger exoplanets orbiting the stars that are closest to us that are the ones we're managing to **detect**. It seems likely that, as our technology gets better, we'll be able to detect smaller exoplanets as well as exoplanets orbiting stars much further away.)

As of 1st February 2019 scientists have found more than

3,950 planets in over 2,950 solar systems, with 653 of these solar systems already known to have more than one planet.

Before we move on, let's take a moment to introduce yet another way of measuring distances. We've already talked about Astronomical Units being more useful than kilometres for measuring and describing large distances with the Solar System. As we move further out into space, the AU measurement becomes less useful. The star Kepler 11, for example, the one with six exoplanets, is a long way from our solar system. In fact it is about 20,340 trillion (that's 20,340,000,000,000,000) km from us. That's about 135,600,000 AU. And, as stars go, that one's quite near us!

So instead of using kilometres or AU for these larger distances, scientists use a different measurement of distance, called the **light-year**. One light-year is the distance that light travels in one year. Light travels at a very high speed (in fact, we don't think that anything can travel faster than light) – its speed is about 300,000 kilometres per second. So a light-year, the distance that light travels in a year, is about 9.46 trillion kilometres.

Don't get confused, mind: a **year** is a measurement of **time**, but a **light-year** is a measurement of **distance**.

The star Kepler 11 we've just talked about is 2,150 light-years away from us. So, travelling at the speed of light (which, as I've said, we think is impossible for anything that isn't light), it would take 2,150 years to get there. In our 'super-fast' 25,000 km per hour space-ship, it would be a nine-million-year journey. Which, let's face it, is a problem if we wanted to pay a visit!

(You can see now why science-fiction movies and TV shows usually have a way for space-ships to travel long distances that involves faster-than-light travel. Otherwise exploring strange new worlds, seeking out new life and new civilisations, and boldly going where no man or woman has gone before would involve an awful lot of time with the crew just sitting around, bored witless. That's boring for them and makes for really boring TV, too!)

Galaxies

Let's continue looking at the building blocks of the universe. We've established that there are lots of stars in the universe, and many probably have their own solar systems, made up of planets, moons, asteroids and other stuff.

If you're thinking that these stars just float about randomly in space, then think again. In fact all the stuff in the universe, the stars, the planets, the clouds of gas and dust, tend to clump together, into 'islands' of matter surrounded by huge empty spaces.

These clumps, or groups of matter, are called **galaxies**.

Our own solar system is part of a galaxy which we call **The Milky Way**. (On a clear night with no moonlight you can sometimes see the Milky Way as a faint strip of light across the sky.)

Galaxies are quite easy to see with powerful telescopes (especially the powerful **Hubble telescope**), but of course we can only look at them from a distance. We can see their large-scale structure quite easily; it's a lot harder to look inside galaxies and see the individual stars that make them up.

A fish-eye view of part of our Milky Way galaxy, seen from planet Earth

Galaxies come in a number of types, named after the way they look. So for example there are **elliptical galaxies** and disc galaxies, which are also known as **spiral galaxies**. A lot of galaxies have strange names, such as the Clouds of Magellan, the Draco dwarf, the Fornax dwarf, Andromeda, the Pinwheel, the Whirlpool, Centaurus A, the Sombrero, and the Zwicky Antennae.

Spiral galaxies tend to be younger galaxies, made up of younger stars and with some stars still being formed. Elliptical galaxies are older. The Milky Way is a spiral galaxy.

Some galaxies are quite small (relatively speaking), whilst other galaxies are quite large. You might want to make sure you're sitting down for the next bit: a 'small' galaxy is made up of about a hundred million stars (yes, 100,000,000) – plus all the planets and other stuff orbiting these stars. A giant galaxy can contain up to a hundred trillion (100,000,000,000,000) stars.

Types of galaxies: top left: spiral (NGC4414, 60 million light-years away); top right: barred spiral (NGC1300, 61 million light-years away); bottom left: a ring galaxy (Hoag's object, 600 million light-years away); bottom right: pinwheel galaxy (NGC5457, 21 million light-years away)

How big are galaxies? Well, we think that the Milky Way (an average-sized galaxy, as far as we can tell) is about 100,000 light years in diameter and has between 200 billion and 400 billion stars. To put that in perspective, if the Sun were the size of a full stop on your page (one of these: .), then the Milky Way would be about 237,000 kilometres across.

Like most galaxies, the Milky Way is rotating. So the Sun, the Earth and all the other couple of hundred billion or so stars in the Milky Way are moving around the centre of the galaxy. In fact the Milky Way is rotating at about 250 kilometres per second, and it takes about 250 million years to make one complete revolution. This is called the **galactic year** (just as the Earth year is the time it takes for the Earth to rotate once around the Sun).

Oh, and in case you are interested, the Milky Way is really nothing special: it's a pretty average galaxy. Our Sun is a pretty average star, too. It's not even near the centre of the Milky Way: it's about half-way out, somewhere in the **suburbs**.

The nearest galaxy to ours is called the **Andromeda Galaxy**. It is about 220,000 light-years across and is about 2.5 million light-years from Earth.

The Andromeda Galaxy, our nearest neighbour. A spiral galaxy, it is about 2.5 million light-years away

If you've still got room in your head to take in some more facts and figures, let me just add this: scientists estimate that the number of galaxies in the **observable universe** (that's just the part of universe that we can see from Earth) is between roughly 200 billion and two trillion. That's a wide range, because it's a very difficult number to estimate accurately. But, any way you look at it, we are talking (yet again!) about very big numbers.

Based on that estimate, how many stars are there in the universe? Well, if there are between a hundred million and a hundred trillion stars in each galaxy, and if there are between 200 billion and two trillion galaxies in the universe, then the **lowest** estimate for the number of stars in the universe would be

100 million x 200 billion = 20 quintillion.

(I bet that's a number you've not met before. It's 20,000,000,000,000,000,000.)

The highest estimate for the number of stars in the universe would be

100 trillion x 2 trillion = 200 septillion.

That's 200,000,000,000,000,000,000,000, 000.

200,000,000,000,000,000, 000,000,000 stars!

I'm told that, whichever of these numbers is correct, there are actually more stars in the universe than there are grains of sand on planet Earth. I can't be sure, though: I haven't checked – and I don't plan to.

By the way, did you notice that I've started talking about the

observable universe. Yes, you've got it – part of the universe is observable (by us): we can see it with powerful telescopes. But we know that there are parts of the universe that we cannot – and cannot *ever* – see. It doesn't matter how powerful our telescopes become in future: we will never see these parts of the universe. Not because our telescopes aren't good enough, but because it would take longer for light to reach us from those parts of the universe than the universe has been in existence. (Remember, light takes time to travel from one place to another.) So, for us, these parts of the universe will remain forever unobservable.

If this is getting a bit hard to follow, don't worry: we'll come back to it in the next chapter.

Galaxy groups and superclusters

If you're thinking that galaxies are the biggest structures in the universe, well … guess what? You're wrong. It seems that, just as stars group together in galaxies, galaxies group together into **galaxy clusters**, or galaxy groups.

Our own Milky Way galaxy is part of a galaxy group we call (not surprisingly) the **Local Group**. This is a group of 54 galaxies, about 10 million light-years across in size.

These galaxy groups then come together to form **superclusters** of galaxies – which we think are actually the biggest structures in the universe. A supercluster is huge; the Local Group galaxy group that we are part of belongs to a supercluster which we call the **Laniakea supercluster**. This supercluster is made up of more than 100,000 galaxies, and is more than 500 million light-years across.

A supercluster of galaxies – a giant group of galaxy clusters which are themselves clustered together. This is Abell 901/902, located just over two billion light-years from Earth. It contains hundreds of galaxies in a region about 16 million light-years across

Superclusters aren't spread out evenly in the universe. They seem to gather in clumps, with huge gaps, or **cosmic voids**, in between the clumps. So, at the large scale, the universe looks a bit like a swiss cheese. And the gaps between superclusters seem to have almost nothing in them: they're like big holes in space.

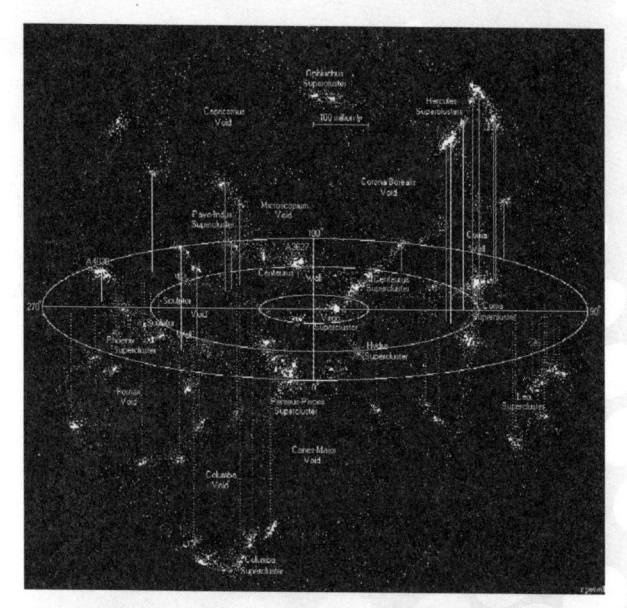

A map of the universe showing most of the superclusters within 500 million light-years of our solar system

What's all this got to do with aliens?

Fascinating as all this information is, we need to keep our focus on getting an answer to our aliens question. There's a couple of important things that we need to take away with us from this chapter.

First of all, we need to understand that the universe is big. **Very big**. There are a lot of stars in the universe, and we know enough about the universe to be sure that many of these stars will probably have planets orbiting them.

We said that the star Kepler 11 has six **exoplanets**; some stars will have more, some less. Even at an average of one planet for each star in the universe, that's still a lot of planets where alien life could be lurking. Based on the estimates for the number of stars in the universe contained in this chapter, there could be around **20 quintillion** planets in the universe.

How many of these planets might actually sustain life is something we'll get to in Chapter Six.

Long distance space travel will bring special problems with it

The second big takeaway from this chapter is the simple fact that, because the universe is so vast, getting around takes **time**. Even at the speed of light (which, as I keep saying, we think is impossible for anything that isn't light), travelling to our nearest galaxy, **Andromeda**, would take two and a half million years. And that's at the speed of light!

In our now rather rubbish-looking 25,000 kph space-ship (43,200 times slower than the speed of light), the same trip would take around 108 billion years.

It's very difficult to think about how humans might plan for such a long journey, even if we had the technology to make it possible. It would mean many millions of **generations** of people in space, somehow able to feed and support themselves (and not go crazy).

There's a much more important problem, too. A 108-billion-year journey to Andromeda would take about seven and a half times longer than the entire time the universe has been in existence. Let's face it, it's hard to set out on a journey tens of billions of years before the place you're leaving and the place you're going to even exist. And you. You don't exist then, either.

Which neatly takes us on to our next topic. In this chapter we've looked at the structure of the universe as it is now. Let's now move on to look at how the universe began, how it is changing and how it might end.

And whether our universe is the only one.

" The universe is simmering down, like a giant stew left to cook for four billion years. Sooner or later we won't be able to tell the carrots from the onions. "

Arthur Bloch

THE HISTORY OF THE UNIVERSE

Where did the universe come from?

Did the universe have a beginning? Was it created in some way? Or has it always been there (or here?) – and if it has, will it continue to be here (or there) forever?

These are very **profound** questions, and throughout the ages people have been asking themselves where the universe and everything in it came from. Of course these questions are about what you *believe* as much as what you can prove, since nobody has been around long enough to know if and how the universe began.

Old ideas about the beginning

For many peoples around the world, stories about how the world began are usually mixed up with stories about how life began, too. These **creation myths** help define how a group of people thinks about itself.

For example the **San** people, who live in the Kalahari Desert of south west Africa, believe that the world (and all life in it) was created by a praying mantis god called Cagn. In the beginning he lived on Earth alongside people, but then he left, disgusted by the foolishness of the human race. Even today the praying mantis is sacred to the people of the Kalahari.

A San tribesman

The **Guarayu-Guarani** people of Bolivia believe that in the beginning, after water and bullrushes had appeared, there was a worm called Mbir, slithering about in the rushes. Then Mbir became a man, and as a man he created the rest of the world out of **chaos**.

The ancient Greeks thought long and hard about how the world was created – and how it was constructed. The ancient Greek philosopher **Aristotle**, who lived from 384 to 322 BCE (remember that before the Common Era, numbers go down as you get older!) has been called the father of modern philosophy.

He thought that the Earth was **stationary** and was at the centre of everything, with the Sun, the Moon, the stars and everything else moving in circular orbits around the Earth. The Earth, said Aristotle, is **immobile**, surrounded by nine **concentric** transparent spheres. Outside that was the sphere of the **Prime Mover**, or Unmoved Mover, who kept it all going.

The Aristotelian **tradition** (yes, he had his own tradition) was that you could work out all the laws that govern the universe by pure thought; you didn't need to check them by **observation**. Aristotle looked down on practical people such as craftsmen and engineers (people who built things), because he thought that their job was done. There was nothing else that could be invented to make life more comfortable. (And this was two thousand years before microwave ovens, TV remotes and the internet!)

The Greek philosopher Aristotle

Because Aristotle was respected as a great thinker, people mostly accepted his view of the world. In fact some of his ideas continued to be accepted for nearly two thousand years, until

Galileo proved them wrong in the sixteenth century with a simple experiment. (Aristotle had said that heavy objects fell to Earth more quickly than lighter objects. Galileo is supposed to have dropped different objects from the top of the leaning Tower of Pisa, showing that they all fell to Earth at the same speed.)

By the way, Aristotle also believed that the universe hadn't been created and it would never end; instead, he said, it would exist unchanging and **static** forever. He also believed that the universe was **finite** in size.

A quiet revolution

Aristotle's **influence** was huge, but in western Europe all ideas about how the world was created came from Christian teaching. God, people said, had created the world in six days, and on the seventh day he had rested. This was accepted **literally**, so there wasn't much left to discuss about how the universe was created. Instead, people focused on thinking about how the universe was *constructed*. How had God built the world?

The story of our changing understanding of the universe over the next two thousand years is fascinating, and features some quite extraordinary thinkers. Let's quickly skim over the surface of the story and mention some of the highlights.

Claudius Ptolemaeus (we call him **Ptolemy**) lived sometime around 150 CE (about 500 years after Aristotle). He lived in the city of Alexandria in Egypt, which at that time was part of the Roman empire. Ptolemy was an astronomer, mathematician, astrologer and geographer, and is most famous for putting together an **encyclopaedia** of mathematics called the **Almagest**. This was a summary of everything that was known at the time about science and mathematics.

Ptolemy

Ptolemy said that the Moon, the Sun and the five planets (only five planets had been discovered by that time) revolved around the Earth in perfect circles. The Earth was at the centre of the universe.

Ptolemy's model of the universe

Why circles? Because people thought that the circle was the perfect form of motion, and God, who designed it all, would not do anything that wasn't perfect.

There was a problem though, because Ptolemy could observe the motions of the Sun, the Moon and the brighter planets such as Mars, and the ways they moved in the sky didn't fit with his model of perfect circles. So he had to fudge it by creating circles moving inside other circles (we call them **epicycles**) to get closer to what he saw happening in the skies. And even then it didn't fit properly.

(By the way, our word *planet* comes from the Greek word for *wanderer*. The planets look like stars, but they seem to wander about in the sky, unlike the stars, which rotate but don't seem to move relative to each other.)

Ptolemy's system needed 39 wheels to move through the sky, plus the 40th wheel at the very outside (the fixed stars). After Ptolemy, this became the accepted model of the universe for nearly 1,500 years (even though it didn't fit what they could see in the night sky!)

Although when **King Alphonso X of Castile** saw Ptolemy's model of the universe in about 1250 CE, he famously said, 'If the Lord Almighty had consulted me

King Alphonso X of Castile

before embarking upon the Creation, I should have recommended something simpler.'

Nicolas Koppernigk, known to us by his Latin name **Copernicus**, was born in 1473 in Torun, in Poland. He studied law and practised medicine later in his life. (What did *medicine* mean in those days? Common medical prescriptions included lemon rind, a deer's heart-bone, a beetle, the horn of a unicorn, lizards boiled in olive oil, earthworms washed in wine, and donkey's urine. These were still dark times.)

Nicolas Copernicus

Copernicus was a bit of a plodder, but in the year he died, (1543 – of a haemorrhage of the brain), his famous book, *On the Revolutions of the Heavenly Orbs*, was published. This book did one hugely dramatic thing: it put the Sun, not the Earth, at the centre of the Solar System and made everything rotate around it. Copernicus had revolutionised our understanding of the heavens at a stroke.

In fact, Copernicus had written his book thirty years earlier, but he'd delayed its publication because he knew that what he was proposing went against the teachings of the Church. In those days, he would probably have been executed for **heresy** just for suggesting that the Earth was not at the centre of everything. So he waited until his dying days, when he knew he wouldn't be around to face the **consequences**. It is said that on his deathbed a copy of his book was brought from the printers for him to hold. What must he have felt at that moment?

Copernicus realised that Ptolemy's model of the universe was all so complicated because we were looking at it all from the wrong place. So he chose a different place: he put the Sun at the centre of the heavens, and made the Earth move around the Sun. He probably put the Sun at centre for emotional reasons, rather than for any reasons of logic.

A diagram from Copernicus' book, On the Revolutions of the Heavenly Orbs. The Sun, labelled 'Sol', is at the centre

Just as in Ptolemy's model though, in Copernicus' model the planets still moved around the Sun in perfect circles, and Copernicus too made use of epicycles to get it all to fit. Nobody was ready, yet, to consider something other than perfect circles. In fact, whilst Ptolemy had 40 circles in his model, Copernicus ended up with 48!

It's hard now to see how **radical** all this was; to the **medieval** mind the Aristotelian Ptolemaic system was a given: it was just how things were. The person in the street, the man in the **pulpit** (always men in those days) and the whole world order depended upon the heavens marching around the Earth.

Yet it was nearly another hundred years before people began to take Copernicus' book seriously.

Johannes Kepler was born in 1571 in what is now Germany. To give you a flavour of how things were in those days, Kepler's mother was an innkeeper's daughter, who was brought up by an aunt who was burnt as a witch. And between 1617 and 1620 Kepler himself was forced to defend his mother when she herself was

Johannes Kepler

Three witches being burnt in the year 1555

tried for **witchcraft**. Kepler's birthplace had a population of two hundred families, yet 38 witches were burnt there between 1615 and 1629. In neighbouring Leonberg (where Kepler's mother was living), six witches were burnt in the winter of 1615 alone. These were bad times!

Kepler was a man of rare skills, combining a love of detail with a search for underlying general scientific principles. He was well-educated and knew Copernicus' theories in detail. Kepler's interest in the heavens came from his letters to and from the great astronomer **Tycho de Brahe**, an eccentric Danish

Tycho de Brahe

nobleman who I have to mention here, if only because he wore a nose made of silver and gold (or perhaps brass), since his own had been sliced off in a duel (in a quarrel over who was the better mathematician!). Who says mathematics isn't dangerous?

Kepler's great idea was to realise that the motion of the planets was not circular and was not uniform. In fact he found that the planets move in an **elliptical** shape, with the planets speeding up and slowing down as they move around the ellipse. The obsession with perfect circular motion was finally abandoned.

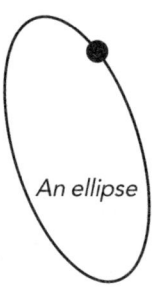

An ellipse

Kepler is also important because he came up with three important mathematical laws describing the motions of the planets. For the first time, we were beginning to do more than just *describe* the heavens: we were trying to *explain* them. Yet Kepler felt ashamed by his first law, since it contained ugly **ellipses** (which were clearly less perfect than circles) and he tried every means possible to avoid having to use them.

Galileo Galilei was born in Pisa, in Italy, in 1564 (the year of Shakespeare's birth and of Michelangelo's death, and seven years before Kepler was born).

Galileo was hired as Professor of Mathematics at Padua, near **Venice**, in 1592, when he was aged just 26. At this time Venice was an important trading port, where **ambitious** merchants and **adventurers** came to seek their fortune. The Mediterranean was the centre of the world and Venice was the hub of the Mediterranean.

Galileo Galilei

Galileo wasn't a dry and dusty professor, though; he was an inventor, too. In 1609, at the age of 45, he built a **telescope** – having heard of a **primitive** spyglass brought from Flanders to Venice. That spyglass had a **magnification** of three. He built one with a magnification of 10, which made it more powerful and more useful. It was a real telescope. With such a device, merchants in Venice could identify a ship more than two hours' sailing time away, which was worth money to them.

But what Galileo did next changed history – and nearly cost him his life. He turned his telescope towards the night sky, and observed four objects (we would call them moons) moving around the planet Jupiter. He could see them pass in front of, and then behind, the giant planet.

In a single moment Galileo could see that not everything orbited the Earth (as Ptolemy's model, still the only explanation allowed by the Church, said it did).

Galileo wasn't Copernicus, though; he was **arrogant** and liked to boast about his **achievements**. A year after first seeing the moons of Jupiter, he published his book, *The Starry Messenger*, which gave an illustrated account of what he had seen. The book caused a sensation.

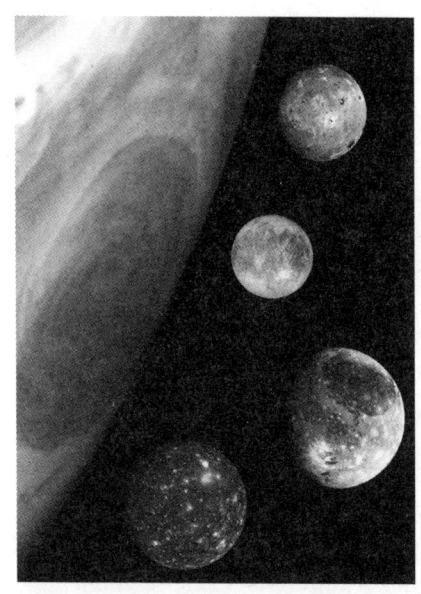

The four moons of Jupiter that Galileo saw, shown next to Jupiter for size

News spread. Galileo thought that all he had to do was show that Copernicus was right (that is, to show that not everything orbited the Earth) and everybody would listen to him and change their theories. Bad mistake: the Church was not happy.

Finally, in September 1634, aged 70 and very ill, Galileo was summoned to Rome to appear before the Holy Office of the **Inquisition**, which had been set up to stamp out 'heretical depravity' (whatever that is!).

There were ten judges at Galileo's trial, and they were all religious leaders. The trial was formal and polite; everybody spoke in Latin and referred to each other as 'he', never 'you' or 'I'. Galileo was politely told to withdraw the statements in his book and (less politely) was shown the instruments of **torture**.

Galileo at his trial before the Inquisition

In those days people were often tortured until they confessed to their 'crimes'. But, for Galileo, seeing the torture instruments was enough; he could imagine the rest. So he agreed to withdraw his statement that the Earth moves around the Sun; he had no choice. (Although as he left the courtroom, Galileo is said to have muttered, 'All the same, it does move'.)

Galileo spent the rest of his life under strict house arrest and died, still a prisoner in his own house, in 1642. On Christmas Day of the same year, in England, Isaac Newton was born.

One final word: in 1992, 359 years after finding Galileo guilty, the Catholic church officially declared that Galileo had been right. The Earth does indeed move around the Sun.

Isaac Newton is a towering genius in the history of science. He was born in Lincolnshire, England, in 1642 and he died in 1727. He discovered gravity (or *invented* it, depending on your point of view – see Chapter Eight!) and he made vital discoveries in many other areas of science, especially concerning light and motion. His three **laws of motion** are still used today.

Isaac Newton

(In 1969, for example, when the US space agency **NASA** first put a man on the Moon, they used Newton's laws of motion to calculate where to point the rocket. Why? Because his laws of motion worked; they made accurate predictions.)

But here, we're going to talk about Newton for two reasons only: his laws of **gravity**, and his role as the creator of what we now call the **scientific method**.

Newton's big mark on history was a book he wrote, published in 1687, usually called the **Principia Mathematica** (*Principles of Mathematics*). It was written in Latin, as all important books of the time were, and it's probably the most important scientific book ever published. Until then it hadn't really occurred to anybody that the universe might actually obey simple, universal, scientific laws.

Rather than just describing how things *are*, Newton tried to discover the **underlying** scientific rules that explain *why* things are the way they are. Any rules like this that we might come up with (such as the idea that the planets orbit the Earth in perfect circles) could then be tested against what we could see happening in the real world. If our rules made correct **predictions**, then they *might* be correct; if reality didn't follow our 'rules', then clearly our rules were wrong. This is what we now call the scientific method.

Newton's way of thinking assumed that we are not looking at a universe that is **static** and unchanging, but rather one that might in fact be changing over time. This was a revolution in thinking about science. For the first time, we were putting forward a set of scientific laws which made the world turn, replacing the belief that everything was constructed at the whim of God. This was really the beginning of the modern age.

It's also worth pointing out that Newton's laws of motion assume that we live in a kind of **clockwork universe**, completely **predictable** and **measurable**. In other words, according to Newton, if we have **accurate** enough information to begin with, we can use his laws of motion to predict exactly how all bodies will move in the future.

Light won't behave

Newtonian mechanics (as scientists called Newton's laws) dominated science until the early 1900s. But by that time a few cracks were beginning to show. In some cases (for example, accurately predicting the orbit of the planet Mercury) Newton's law's were giving results that did not match what we could actually see.

Newton had assumed that somewhere in the universe there was an **absolute** benchmark, like a master clock, against which everything else could be measured. In other words, he assumed that there had to be something in the universe that was either not moving at all, or was always moving at a constant speed. Then everything could be measured relative to that.

Well let's try a little **thought experiment**. Let's think about a person standing at the side of a road next to a railway track. She sees a train pass her, travelling at 100 kilometres per hour, followed by a car on the road travelling at 99 kilometres per hour in the same direction.

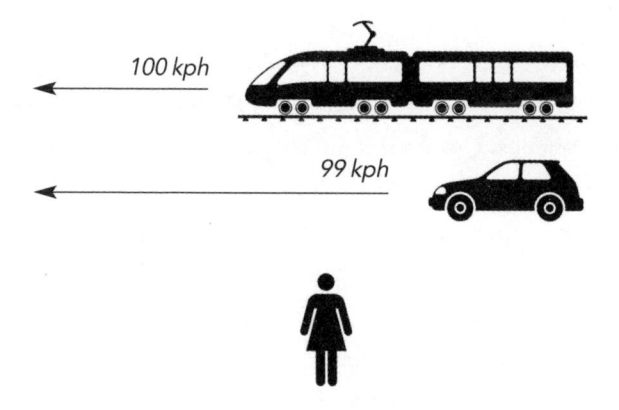

100 kph

99 kph

To a person in the car, the train will be moving away from them at one kilometre per hour – the difference between the speed of the train and the speed of the car.

Now, let's replace the train with a light beam travelling at the speed of light, and the car with a spaceship travelling at, say, half the speed of light.

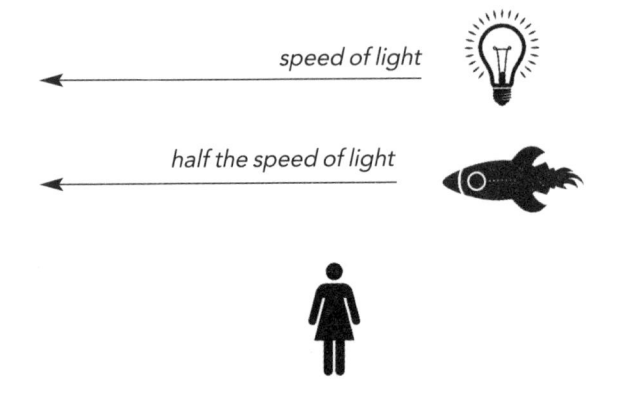

speed of light

half the speed of light

To a person in the space-ship, how fast would the beam of light seem to be moving away from them? You'd expect it to be half of the speed of light, wouldn't you? (That's the speed of light of the light beam, minus half the speed of light – the speed that the space-ship is travelling at.) But no, it's not. The light beam is moving away from the space-ship at exactly the speed of light! We know this, because scientists have carried out the experiment and measured the differences in speed.

Now, let's increase the speed of the spaceship to 99.99% of the speed of light. How fast will the person in the spaceship now see the light beam moving away from them? Again, we'd expect it to be 0.01% of the speed of light (that is, the speed of light minus 99.99% of the speed of light). But it isn't. It's still the speed of light.

To the person at the side of the road, the light beam will also be travelling away from her at the speed of light.

This seems to be just plain silly! How can the stationary person *and* the speeding spaceship both measure the speed of the light beam as being exactly the same?

In fact, to all observers in the universe, the speed of light is *always* the same, no matter whether the observer is moving or not. This was predicted by **James Clerk Maxwell** in 1865 in his theory of **electromagnetism**, and has since been proved in a number of experiments.

James Clerk Maxwell

Wherever you are in the universe, no matter how fast you are moving and no matter in which direction, the speed of light will always be the same: for you – and for everybody else.

For the speed of light, Newton's laws of motion were just plain incorrect. Something was seriously wrong.

Albert Einstein is the second great scientist of the last five hundred years, standing alongside Isaac Newton. Born in 1879, Einstein showed himself to be a clever mathematician from a very young age. In 1903 he found himself working as a humble **patent** clerk, in an office in Bern in Switzerland.

It was around this time that he asked himself a very simple question: 'What would happen if I rode on a beam of light?' (It's always the simple questions that are the hardest to answer!)

Albert Einstein in 1921

Well, let's try to answer it. Say you ride on a beam of light that leaves a clock at exactly twelve o'clock. Now, one second, or one minute, later you look back at the clock. What do you see?

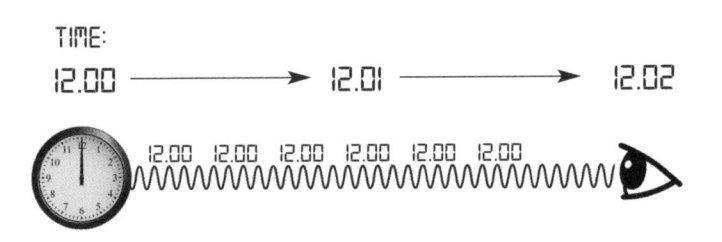

TIME:
12.00 ⟶ 12.01 ⟶ 12.02

12.00 12.00 12.00 12.00 12.00 12.00

Well, to you, the clock will still say twelve o'clock. Why is that? Because you are travelling on the light beam that is moving from the clock that is saying twelve o'clock, that carries that piece of information. No other light beams showing a later time (say one second past twelve), can ever catch up with you.

In other words, if you are travelling at the speed of light, you are completely cut off from the passage of time. For you, time will have stopped completely.

That is startling.

What it also means is that, as you get closer to the speed of light, time will slow down for you. In addition, you will also get physically smaller and much, much heavier.

If you are travelling at a tenth of the speed of light, your mass (what you weigh) is about half a percent more than usual. Travelling at 90% of the speed of light, your mass is doubled. And at the speed of light itself, your mass would be infinite – and you'd need infinite energy to reach that speed. (Which is of course impossible.)

This is Einstein's **theory of relativity**. As you get closer to the speed of light, time slows down, distances reduce and mass increases, said Einstein. Newton was wrong: there is no universal time.

Einstein also had a different explanation for **gravity**. Newton had said that gravity is a force acting at a distance, which is why the Earth and the Sun attract each other. It's why the Earth goes around the Sun and doesn't fly off into space.

But Einstein said something very different. He said that space and time are linked, into something that he called **space-time**.

Space-time is like a rubber sheet, and objects **distort** space-time by curving the rubber sheet. Heavier objects curve the sheet more than lighter objects. It's just like when you stand on a trampoline; your weight distorts the rubber sheet.

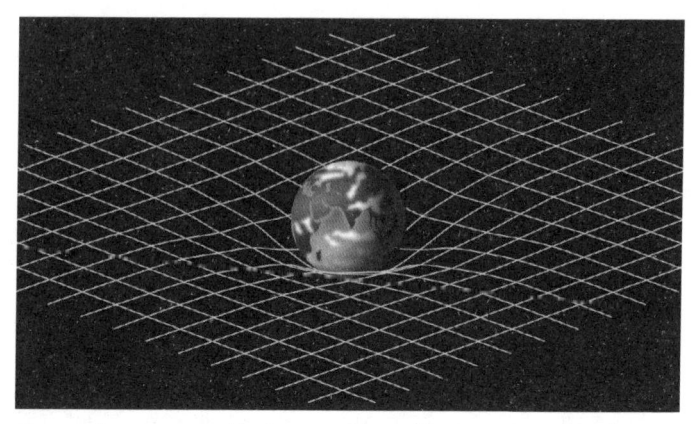

Space-time is curved by heavy objects like our planet Earth

So for Einstein, gravity is the way that space-time is distorted by the **presence** of matter. And the heavier the object is, the more space-time is distorted.

Think of a heavy object like the Sun bending the rubber sheet. If a lighter object, say a planet, moves along the sheet in a straight line, it won't actually travel in a straight line. Rather, the **curvature** of space-time will cause it to move in a circular path around the heavy object. The planet is actually following a straight line – but in curved space.

To get the idea, ask a friend to stand on a trampoline and then try to roll a tennis ball past their feet in a straight line. You won't be able to – the tennis ball will roll into the dip and settle at your friend's feet.

Are Einstein's theories correct? Well they have been tested in experiments and so far he's been proved right. And his theory of gravity can explain the bits that Newton's theory couldn't, such as accurately explaining the orbit of the planet Mercury.

So if Einstein is right and Newton is wrong, why do we still use Newton's laws? Why do we still learn them in school? Well, because for most cases in the real world, Newton's laws are accurate enough to be right. And the maths is a lot easier to do than Einstein's equations!

The expanding universe

By the early 1920s the scientific world was reeling as a result of Einstein's theories. Then came another huge shock.

Edwin Hubble is probably one of the least-known names amongst modern scientists, but for us, trying to understand why we haven't seen aliens, he is very important. (And yes, the **Hubble telescope** is named after him.)

Edwin Powell Hubble (1889 - 1953) was the American son of a lawyer. He took degrees in mathematics and astronomy at the University of Chicago and then went to Oxford to study law. After taking his law degree at Oxford he returned to the USA to practise law, until he joined the staff of the Yerkes Observatory in 1914. In the next few

Edwin Hubble

decades Hubble carried out very important work looking at galaxies and the large scale structure of our universe.

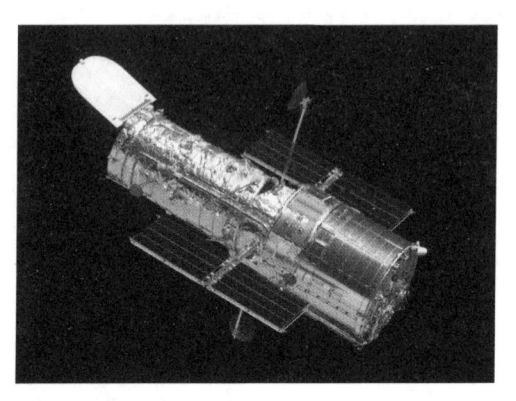

The Hubble space telescope is named after Edwin Hubble

At that time scientists knew about the Milky Way galaxy, but they thought that the whole universe was made up of just this one galaxy. But in 1924 Hubble showed that the Milky Way was not the only galaxy, and that there were many others – all with huge areas of empty space between them. This was a shock; the universe was obviously much, much bigger than we had previously thought.

Then in 1929 Hubble also discovered that, wherever you look in the universe, most galaxies are moving away from us at high speed. And even more strange – the further away from us these galaxies are, the faster they are moving away from us. In fact Hubble found a simple mathematical relationship between a galaxy's distance from us and its speed. This is now called **Hubble's law**.

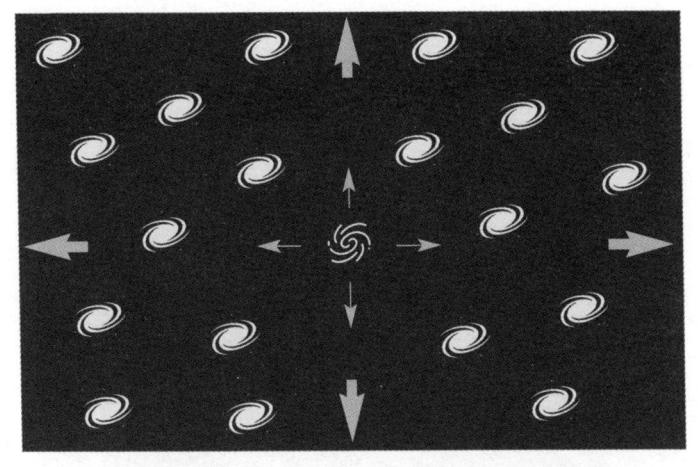

Hubble discovered that galaxies are moving away from us at high speed. The further away from us a galaxy is, the faster it is moving away from us

This was all revolutionary stuff – and it wasn't a *theory*, it was based on what Hubble had actually seen. But what did it mean? It seemed pretty obvious that we don't live in a static and unchanging universe after all! Clearly the universe is expanding, with everything moving away from everything else at high speed.

(This isn't *quite* true. Some galaxies are moving towards each other. For example the Andromeda Galaxy and our own Milky Way seem to be heading towards each other at high speed – although they probably won't collide for a few billion years yet.)

It's also worth noting that, despite what he discovered, Hubble refused to believe that the universe actually was expanding. He kept trying to find other explanations – but without success.

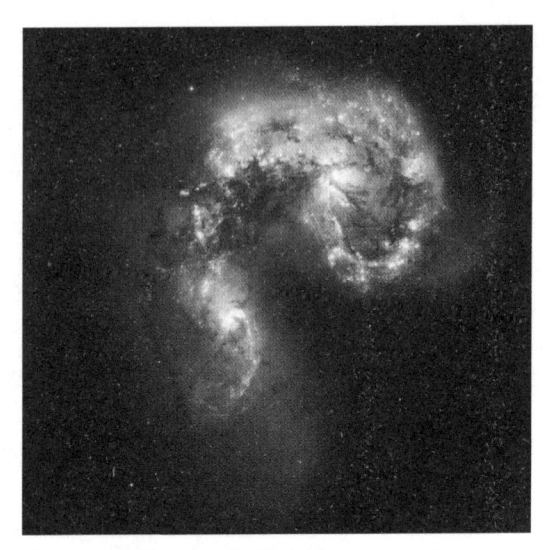

An image taken by the Hubble space telescope of two galaxies colliding. These are called the Antennae Galaxies, also known as NGC 4038 and NGC 4039

The Big Bang

After the shock of Hubble's findings about the universe and Einstein's theories about gravity, scientists started to think about the history of the universe. Did it have a beginning, and if so, how had it begun?

Basically there were two theories: steady state and big bang. Arguments between supporters of the two theories became quite heated! The **Steady State theory** said that the universe had always existed and will always exist. Yes, the universe was expanding, supporters of the theory said – they couldn't argue with that, since Hubble had proved it – but new matter was being created to fill in the gaps as the universe expanded. Where was this matter coming from? Well, said supporters of the theory, it was just appearing.

The biggest supporter of the Steady State theory was the English scientist (and science fiction writer) **Sir Fred Hoyle**, who had suggested the theory in 1948. In fact Hoyle was the one who came up with the name 'Big Bang' to describe the alternative theory. (He thought the Big Bang theory was a silly theory, so he gave it a silly name.)

Two competing theories

The alternative theory, the **Big Bang theory**, said that the universe had begun from a single point at a single time, from which everything had started.

Supporters of this theory said that if Hubble was right, and if the universe is expanding as we move forward in time into the future, then, if we could somehow play the 'movie' of the universe backwards (mathematically at least), we would see the universe get smaller and smaller as we moved further back into the past.

Big Bang

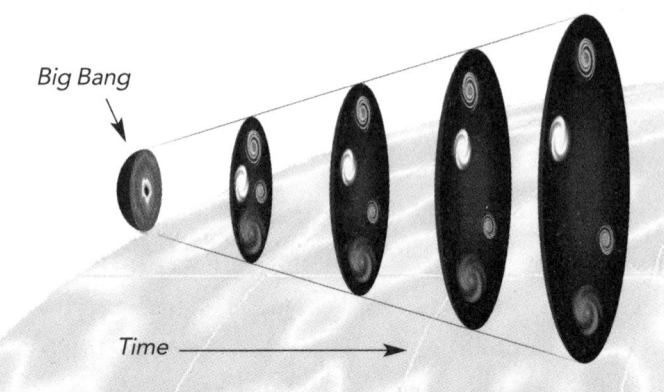

Time ⟶

The Big Bang theory: following a 'big bang', the universe is expanding

If you kept going, eventually at some point in the distant past everything in the universe would have collapsed to a single point. Playing the universe 'movie' forwards from that moment, the universe would have started with what looked like a 'big bang'.

In the 1950s and early 1960s debate raged about which of these two theories was correct. Overall, the Steady State theory was probably more popular, as it seemed to make more sense and was easier to work with mathematically. The idea of the Big Bang seemed to make no sense at all.

One thing nearly everybody accepted, though, was that if the Big Bang had actually happened, then there would have been a lot of heat and light produced at the time (just as you'd expect from a big bang). So even now, about 13 billion years later, it should still be possible to detect some of this heat left over from the Big Bang. This signal would be very weak but, if it existed, we ought to be able to find it. So where was it? The hunt was on!

And then in 1964 two American physicists, **Arno Penzias** and **Robert Wilson**, found this signal. It was coming from all directions of the sky and did not vary with the time of day, or season. The scientists thought at one point that the noise might be caused by pigeons nesting in their radio telescope, but no: it was the leftover **energy** from the Big Bang explosion. We now call it the **cosmic background radiation**.

That was the end for the Steady State theory. The Big Bang theory had won.

The COBE satellite

There's another important part to the story of the cosmic background radiation. Between 1989 and 1993 a satellite (called **COBE**, for **COsmic Background Explorer**) was launched to collect **data** and measure the cosmic background radiation.

The illustration on the next page shows the data collected by the satellite, mapped for the whole of the visible universe. The light and dark parts show where the radiation is higher or lower in different parts of the universe. Scientists think these **fluctuations** reflect **variations** in the universe just after the Big Bang itself.

So our current theory is that the universe started with a 'Big Bang' a long time ago, when everything in the universe started at

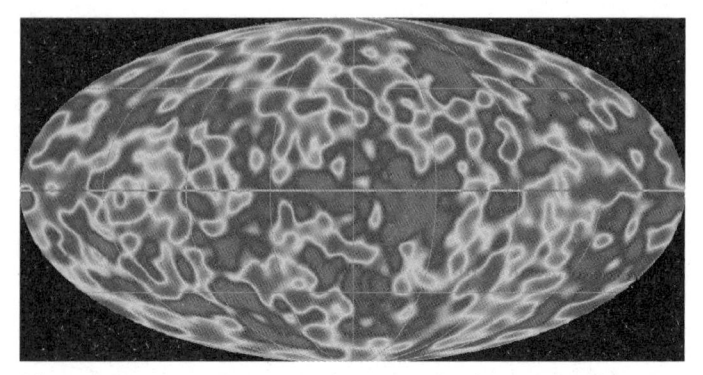

Fluctuations, or variations, in the cosmic background radiation

a single point in space. Scientists call that point a **singularity**.

Winding the 'movie' back, we can calculate that the Big Bang happened about 13.79 billion years ago – which is the figure we use now to describe the age of the universe. At that time the universe would have been **infinitesimally** small and **infinitely dense**.

Scientists now have a pretty good 'model' of how the universe has evolved and changed since the Big Bang.

The first stars and galaxies only began to form after about 500 million years, and these gradually began to clump together into galaxies. From about 1 billion years after the Big Bang up until the present, the universe has looked pretty much as it is now.

Picture right: part of an image taken by the Hubble telescope. Each light speck is a galaxy and some of these galaxies are as old as 13.2 billion years. There are about 10,000 galaxies in this complete image

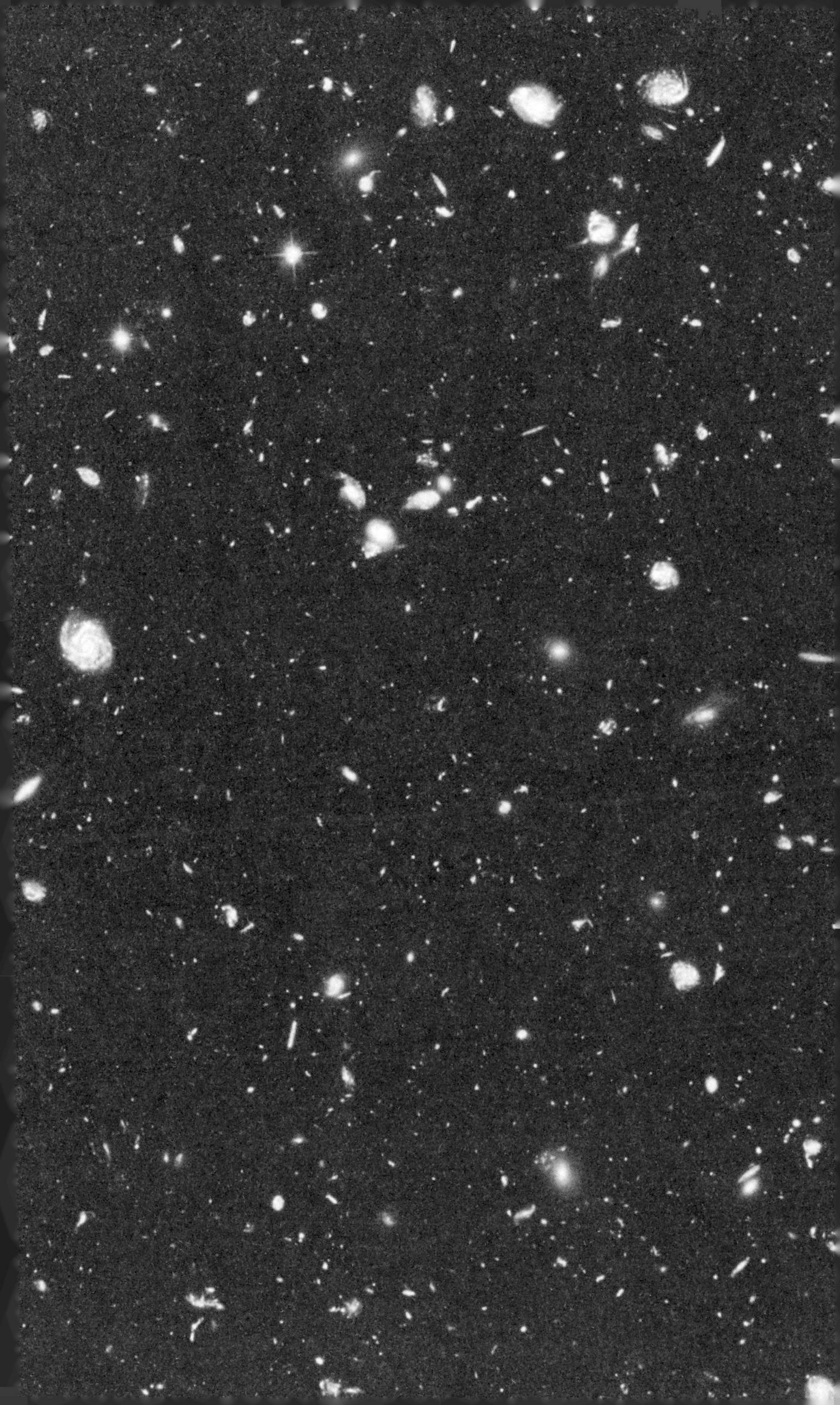

Is the universe infinite?

Infinite things go on forever. Numbers, for example, are infinite. What's the biggest number you can think of? Is there a number that's bigger than that?

Yes, always, because whatever number you think of, you can always add one to make a number that's bigger than the one you thought of. **+1**

Think about all the **even** numbers (2, 4, 6, 8 and so on). Are the even numbers infinite? Yes, because whatever even number you think of, you can always add two and make an even number that's bigger than the one you thought of. **+2**

Now think about all the **odd** numbers (1, 3, 5, 7 and so on). Are the odd numbers infinite? Yes, again, because whatever odd number you think of, you can always add two and make an odd number that's bigger than that. **+2**

Now think about all the odd and even numbers together (1, 2, 3, 4, 5, 6, 7 and so on). Are these numbers infinite? Yes again, because whatever number you think of, you can always add one and make a number that's bigger than that.

Now let's try a **thought experiment**. Let's assume that we put all the even numbers in a box and label it **Box E**. Then we put all the odd numbers in a box and label it **Box O**. Then we put *all* the numbers (all the odd numbers and all the even numbers together) in a box called **Box I**.

Now, which box has the most numbers in it? Do I hear you say **Box I**? After all, it has not just the odd numbers or just the even

Box E
even

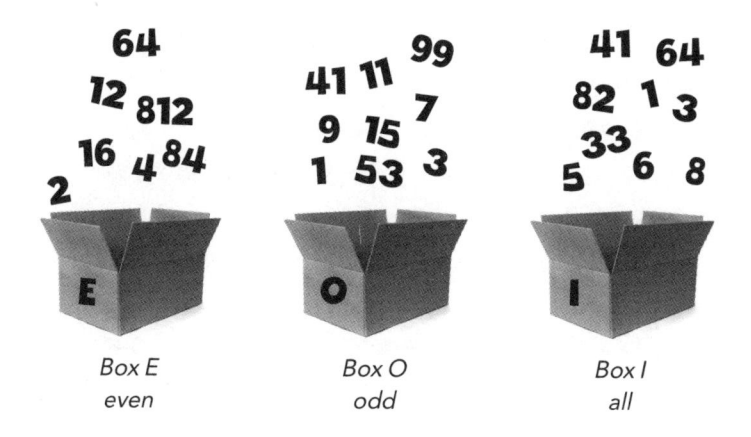

Box O
odd

Box I
all

numbers, but ALL numbers, both odd and even, in it. So it must have the most numbers in it.

But no. That's not true. In fact, all three boxes have the same number of numbers in them. And the number of numbers in each box is … infinite! Just think about that for a moment; we are saying that the number of even numbers, for example, is the same as the number of even numbers and the number of odd numbers added together.

Infinity can be a very slippery idea to work with!

So is the universe infinite? In 1823 the German astronomer **Heinrich Olbers** pointed out that if the universe was infinite, then everywhere you looked in the night sky would end on a star or a galaxy. (Because an infinite universe would go on forever, then ending at a star or a galaxy was inevitable). Therefore the night sky would be as bright as daytime, full of light from stars. So the big question was, *Why is the night sky dark?* This question is now called **Olbers' paradox**.

One answer to this that the writer **Edgar Allan Poe** came up with was that if the universe had a beginning in time, and was not therefore infinitely old, then light from the most distant stars might not have reached us yet, but might still be speeding towards us. Hence the night sky is dark (except for the stars whose light we can see).

So if the universe is infinite, what does that actually mean? That it goes on forever? That there is no end, no edge? (If there is an edge, what's on the other side of the edge?) Is there an infinite number of planets, stars and galaxies to fill the infinite universe? If that is the case, does that mean that the Big Bang started 13.8 billion years ago with an infinite amount of stuff? Surely not.

At the moment, we don't really have answers to any of these questions.

There is another way we can think about an infinite universe. Think of a bug walking on the surface of an apple. If it keeps walking in a straight line, it'll never come to an edge, or a stop. It will go on forever, round and round and round the apple.

Does that mean that the surface of the apple is infinite? Well it's a normal-sized apple, but the surface doesn't have an edge. The bug can walk forever and never find the 'edge'. The apple has a **curved surface**.

Some scientists think that the space of the universe itself is curved, like an apple. So if you keep travelling in the universe for long enough, like the bug, you'll get back to where you started. It would take a long time, though: longer than the entire age of the universe! But in theory, some scientists say, you could do it.

How big is the universe?

Scientists think that the **observable universe** – that part of the universe that we can see – is a bit more than 46 billion light-years in any direction from Earth. So that would make the diameter of the observable universe about 93 billion light-years.

The problem is that we are pretty sure that there are parts of the universe that cannot ever be seen from Earth. This isn't because our telescopes aren't powerful enough, but because distant parts of the universe are moving away from us very quickly – and, if you remember, Einstein's **theory of relativity** says that the speed of light, although very high, is finite.

Parts of the universe might be expanding faster than light

Scientists think that the diameter of the observable universe is about 93 billion light-years

can actually cross it. So light from these parts of the universe will never reach us. We can't travel to, or send messages to, those parts of the universe and they can't interact with us either.

Just stop and think about that for a moment.

Our aliens

In this chapter we have moved through over 2,000 years of thinking about science, from a time when people believed that everything moved around the Earth in perfect circles, and the stars were attached to a fixed circular shell around the Earth, to our current understanding of the expanding, ever-changing universe.

So where are we now? And what are the **implications** of our findings in this chapter for our search for alien life? Can they help us explain why we haven't seen aliens?

Let's quickly summarise where we are.

- We believe that the universe began about 13.8 billion years ago, with a **Big Bang**.
- Stars and galaxies did not begin to form until about 500 million to 1 billion years after the Big Bang. That's, say, about 13 billion years ago.
- The universe is **expanding**. Very distant parts of the universe are moving away from us very, very quickly. Parts of the universe might actually be expanding faster than light can cross it.

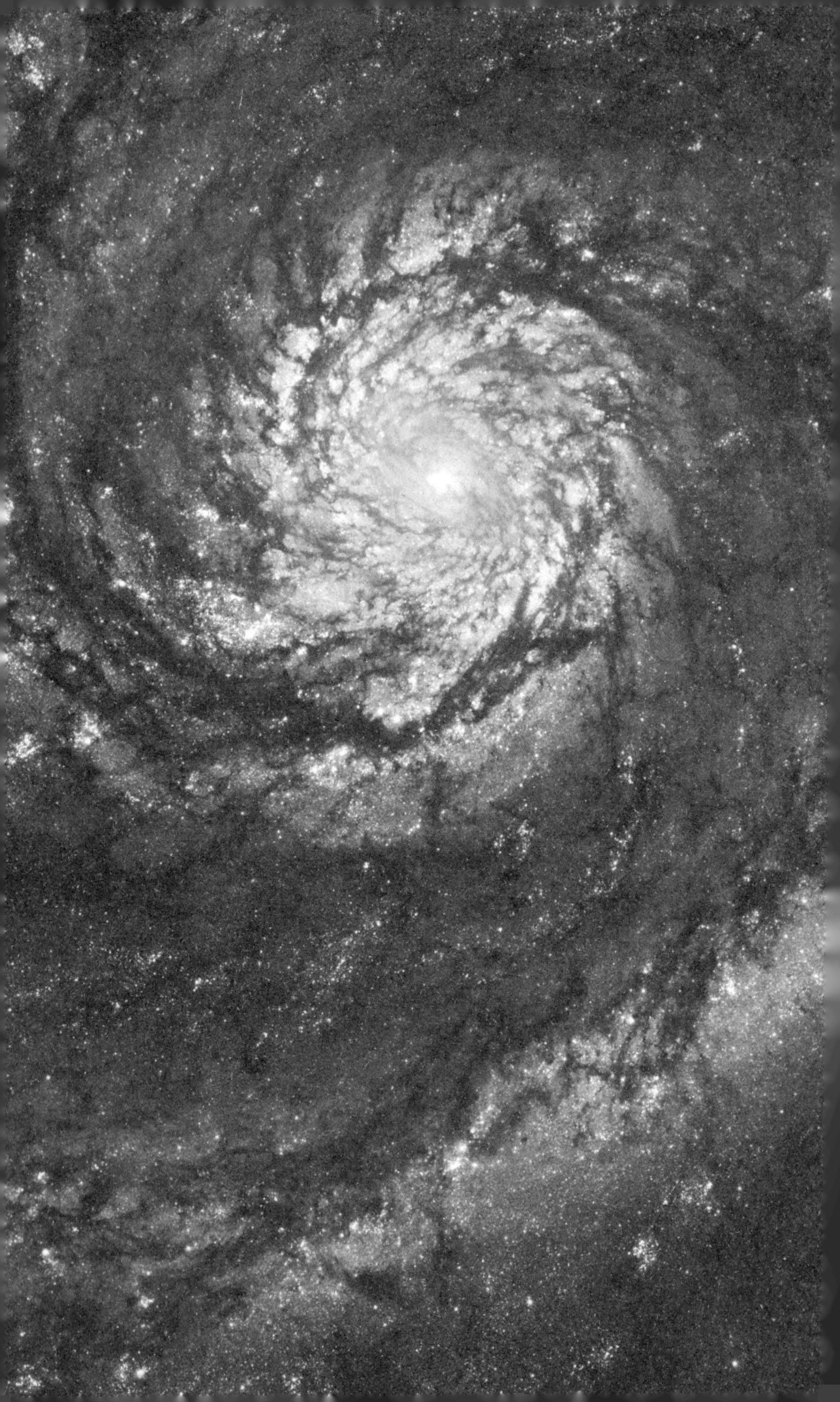

* The universe is **big**. Very, very big. Scientists think the observable universe might be 93 billion light-years in diameter. If we wanted to make a journey of that distance (say to cross from one 'side' of the universe to the other), even if we were travelling at the speed of light, it would take 93 billion years – which is six and a half times longer than the entire age of the universe!

You have probably realised by now that all this could make it very difficult for any aliens who might be lurking out there and might want to get in touch. It makes *our* search for them more difficult, too!

In the next chapter we are going to move on, to look at something else that has a big impact on the chances of our meeting aliens. That something is **life**: what it is, where it comes from and what it needs to survive.

Because understanding more about life will put us in a much better position to come up with some serious answers to our question, 'Why haven't we seen aliens?'

Picture left: the wonders of the universe. The spiral galaxy M51, known as the Whirlpool Galaxy. Hundreds of tiny clumps of stars, each about 65 light-years across, are surrounded by dense dust clouds. Photograph taken by the Hubble Space Telescope

❝ Programming today is a race between software engineers striving to build bigger and better idiot-proof programs, and the universe trying to produce bigger and better idiots. So far, the universe is winning. ❞

Rich Cook

5

LIFE

If we're going to think about the chances of our actually meeting real, living aliens, we need to look a little more closely at this thing we call life.

The questions we really need answers to are these:

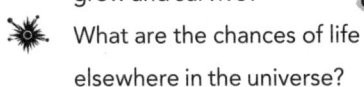

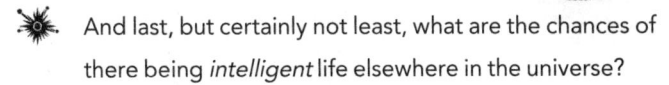

- What is life?
- How did (or does) life start?
- What is needed for living things to grow and survive?
- What are the chances of life elsewhere in the universe?
- And last, but certainly not least, what are the chances of there being *intelligent* life elsewhere in the universe?

Because in order for aliens to travel to planet Earth and ask to be taken to our leader, they're going to need some fairly **advanced** technology. In fact, they'll need technology that is much more advanced than we humans have managed to develop so far on Earth.

Left: astronaut Buzz Aldrin on the Moon, 1969.
Right: the Curiosity rover on the planet Mars, 2015

The furthest from Earth that we have managed to travel to is our moon, which is only 384,400 kilometres away. We have sent unmanned probes much further out into space (to just beyond the edge of our solar system, in fact), but nobody was travelling on them.

That's not really interstellar travel is it?

What is life?

We all pretty much know what living things are when we see them. Ducks, trees, people, dogs, birds, spiders – they're all living things; they are examples of life. Just as mobile phones, bicycles, rocks and ping-pong balls are non-living things. Not life.

But believe it or not, it's quite hard to come up with a definition of 'life'. It's not something that scientists easily agree about.

One definition says that something is living if it can do all of these seven things:

1. **Reproduction** Living things reproduce; they make copies of themselves. (We call them 'babies'.) Sometimes they make exact copies; sometimes the copies are a little bit different.
2. **Growth** Living things grow. They get bigger, making new living material for themselves.
3. **Nutrition** Living things take in stuff (we call it 'food') from outside their 'bodies' and use it to give them the energy they need to do the things on this list.
4. **Respiration** Living things convert the food into the energy they need. They do this inside their cells.
5. **Excretion** Growth, nutrition and respiration produce side products. The ones that can't be used are got rid of by the body. This is excretion.
6. **Senses** Anything that's alive – and is going to stay alive – needs to know about the world around it. It needs

senses of some kind. ('Where's food? Where are the things that want to eat me?')

7   **Locomotion** Being able to move is pretty useful, even if it only means bending your leaves towards the Sun.

This isn't a perfect **definition** and some scientists disagree with parts of it. But it's good enough for our purposes.

Even so, there are still a few examples of things where we aren't sure whether they are living or not. The biggest example is the virus.

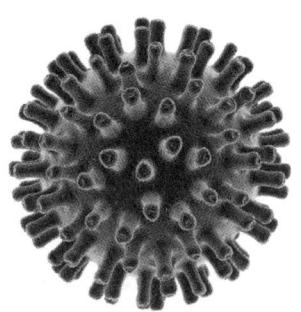

A **virus** is a tiny 'thing' that behaves in most ways as if it were alive. (Viruses really are small; you'd need between about 30,000 and 750,000 viruses, side by side, to stretch to one centimetre. They are too small to see, even with a microscope.)

Viruses are too small to see. A computer image of a virus

Viruses have **genes**, like living things, and they can reproduce and they can evolve. But here's the thing: viruses can only survive inside the living cells of another living thing (we say **organism**.) For many scientists that's the deciding factor: viruses aren't living because they can only 'live' inside other organisms.

We all have viruses inside the cells of our bodies. Usually they cause us no harm, but sometimes viruses can make us ill. The common cold is a virus, for example.

Evolution

Everywhere we look on planet Earth, we see signs of life. Life is all around us – on land, in deserts, at the tops of mountains, under the ground, in the sea, at the bottom of the sea, in the air … life is everywhere.

Life is everywhere

If we look just at insects, for example, biologists think there are between six and ten million different kinds (we call them **species**) of insect. There are so many different kinds, we don't even know how many! Where did so many species come from?

For a long time it was a big puzzle to explain how life on Earth had become so varied. We know from looking at the **fossil record** that most kinds of animals that have lived on Earth at some point have now died out completely. They have become **extinct**. (Think of the dinosaurs!)

Why did all these species die out?

Left: a Megalosaurus dinosaur. Right: a Tarbosaurus. Both are now extinct

The answer to the puzzle came in the form of a theory called **evolution**. Evolution explains how different species of plants and animals change or die out over long, long periods of time.

Evolution was first suggested in 1859 by **Charles Darwin** in his book *Origin of Species*. Since then the theory has been filled in with lots more detail. Evolution is now one of the most powerful explanations in science, and it's accepted by nearly all serious scientists. In fact, the more we find out, the more evidence for evolution there is.

Evolution is a topic that's much too complicated for us to talk about here in any detail. So we're just going to look at the important parts of the theory, to help us understand how life might have started on Earth, and how life changes over time.

Charles Darwin

Evolution in a nutshell

The theory of evolution is in fact very simple. It's a bit like a mathematical equation, or **algorithm**. Basically, evolution occurs whenever you get the following three things.

1. **Reproduction** This is where living things are able to make copies of themselves. So, for example, animals have babies, seedlings grow from plants and bacteria produce more bacteria. (Remember, reproduction was on our list of seven requirements for life, listed at the beginning of this chapter.)
2. **Variation** When living things make copies of themselves, the copies will usually be a little bit different

to the parents. They will **vary**. So children often grow up looking a bit like one (or both) of their parents, but they never look *identical* to their parents. They always look like a different person.

We have a very good understanding of how this works – it's all about the child's **genes** being a combination of some of the mother's and some of the father's genes. And for each child, the combination is always different (except for identical twins, where it's the same).

3 **Natural selection**

Let's explain this by thinking about a field that has both rabbits and foxes living in it. Let's assume that the foxes feed on the rabbits, so to get food to eat, a fox needs to catch and eat a rabbit.

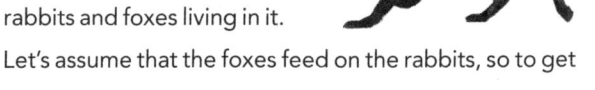

If there are quite a lot of foxes in the field, but not enough rabbits to go round, some of the foxes won't be able to get anything to eat.

Which foxes will go hungry? Well, if all the foxes are trying to catch a rabbit, it will be the strongest foxes, the fastest runners (or perhaps the cleverest foxes), who will manage to catch a rabbit. The weakest, or not-so-clever foxes won't catch any. If this shortage of rabbits continues, in the end the weaker foxes will die of hunger, leaving only the stronger (or cleverer) ones left.

This is called natural selection. Sometimes we say **survival of the fittest**.

The important thing to understand is that, if only the fastest and strongest foxes survive, it will be the fastest and strongest foxes that mate with other fastest and strongest foxes and have babies. So their babies are *likely* to be faster and stronger too (because genes for 'faster' and 'stronger' are being passed on to the fox babies).

And so it will go on, with the faster and stronger babies of these fox babies being more likely to survive.

That's the simplest way of explaining how evolution works. Now notice: if we have these three things going on in a group of living things – replication, variation and natural selection – then evolution *will* happen, over a long, long time. It is **inevitable**. It can't *not* happen.

But evolution makes no sense unless you understand the huge amount of time that there's been for it to take place. Life started on Earth about **three and a half billion years** ago. That's a very, very long time for many millions of generations of organisms to change, very, very slowly.

Evolution explains, for example, how some dinosaurs manage to evolve into birds (again over a very, very long time). The dinosaurs didn't become birds overnight. Rather, over many millions of years, lots of tiny changes added up to new species. We say the birds are **descended** from dinosaurs.

Here are two neat little examples of how evolution works.

The peppered moth

This moth is very common in the United Kingdom. Up until the early 1800s, the moths always had light-coloured wings (the colour of pepper). These wings blended in very well

The original peppered moth

when the moth was resting on a tree, for example. The wings were good **camouflage**.

If a black-winged peppered moth was ever born, it would be easy for birds to spot it, and they would quickly eat it. So light-winged moths **thrived** and mated with other light-winged moths, giving more light-winged moth babies.

But in the 1800s the industrial revolution happened across the UK, with lots of factories being built, and many parts of the country became very polluted. Trees became

The black-winged peppered moth

blackened with soot and dirt. Suddenly the light-winged moths were the ones that were easy to spot; the black-winged moths that were occasionally born were now the ones that were harder for birds to spot. As a result, more light-winged moths were spotted and eaten by birds. Quite quickly, there were far more black-winged moths than light-winged moths. And those black-winged moths mated with other black-winged moths, which produced more black-winged moth babies.

In 1811 black-winged moths were unknown. But by 1895, after the industrial revolution, about 98% of peppered moths had black wings.

Light-winged and black-winged peppered moths on a pollution-free tree. The light-winged moth is harder to spot

So a change in the **environment** where these moths lived meant that white-winged moths weren't the best at surviving any more: the black-winged moths found it easier to survive and they became much more common. In just 100 years or so, almost the whole **population** of these moths had pretty much changed their wing colour.

Clever bugs

A type of bug called a **periodic cicadia** spends almost its **entire** life underground. It only appears above ground for about four to six weeks every 13 years (or every 17 years, depending on the species of cicadia it is). What is amazing is that all the cicadias

A periodic cicadia

appear at the same time, and then disappear together until they all appear again, 13 or 17 years later.

Why every 13 or 17 years? Why not every two or every three years? Nobody knows for sure. But here is a very good suggestion.

There might be an animal (a **predator**) that feeds on the cicadias, and it might come to the place where the cicadias appear, in order to feed on them. If the cicadias appeared every two years, for example, they would be eaten by any predator that came to that place every one, two, four, or six years, and so on.

If the cicadias appeared every three years, they would be eaten by any predator that came every year, every three years, every six years, or every nine years, and so on. If the cicadias appeared, say, every 16 years, then they would meet any predators that came to that place every one, two, four, eight or 16 years.

But 13 and 17 are both **prime numbers**. A prime number is a number that can only be divided by one and itself. (1 × 13 = 13. Nothing else multiples to give 13.) Cicadias that appear every 17 years, for example, will only meet predators that come either every year or every 17 years. Predators that visit every three years will meet the 17-year cicadias in the first year and then not again for 51 years. So 13-year gaps and 17-year gaps are good 'choices' to reduce the chances of getting eaten.

Did the cicadias *choose* to appear every 13 or 17 years? Of course not. More likely, the cicadias that appeared, say, every two years, or every three years, were eaten more often. The 13-year and 17-year cicadias met predators less often, and not so many of them were eaten. These cicadias had a definite advantage – which makes a big difference over time.

Evolution is blind

Next time you go down to the sea, try to find a beautiful pebble on the beach. It has been worn smooth over many thousands of years by the constant wear of the tides, the sea and the wind. The pebble is like it is because of the effects of the sea.

Now, ask yourself, was the pebble *designed* by the sea?

Well, it was made like it is by the processes of tides, winds, and water, for sure. But would we actually say it was *designed* by the sea? Isn't that a strange use of the word 'designed'?

Design usually implies some kind of **intention**, and we'd hardly say that the sea *intended* to shape that pebble. The processes of tides and water made the pebble the way it is, but they didn't design it.

Well, evolution's the same. Evolution is like the sea, and all the creatures on our planet are like pebbles. We are a result of the **processes** of evolution, of random changes and of natural selection. But evolution didn't *design* us: it didn't intend to make us the way we are. **Evolution is blind**: it cannot see what is happening and there is no end result in mind, no intention.

What about the eye?

'Ah,' say the critics of evolution. 'How do we get something as complicated as the human eye (or any other animal's eye), even in three and a half billion years, just by small random changes? That's impossible! The eye must have been designed by somebody.'

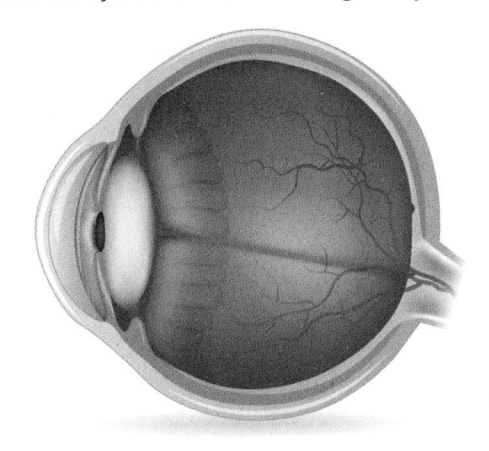

A cross-section of the human eye

Asking the question in this way assumes that our eyes appeared from nowhere, in a single step. In other words, one moment a species doesn't have any eyes – it is completely blind – but then suddenly it has **offspring** that have eyes, that can see.

Put that way, of course it is silly; it's ridiculous. But that isn't how evolution works.

Let's think of a primitive creature that might live in the ocean. Let's say it can move about a little bit, but not very much, and moving about uses lots of energy. So it doesn't want to move about when it doesn't need to.

Let's assume that this creature has no eyes and can't see at all. It lives in a world of total darkness.

What if a random change in one of this creature's offspring meant that the offspring suddenly had a few cells somewhere on

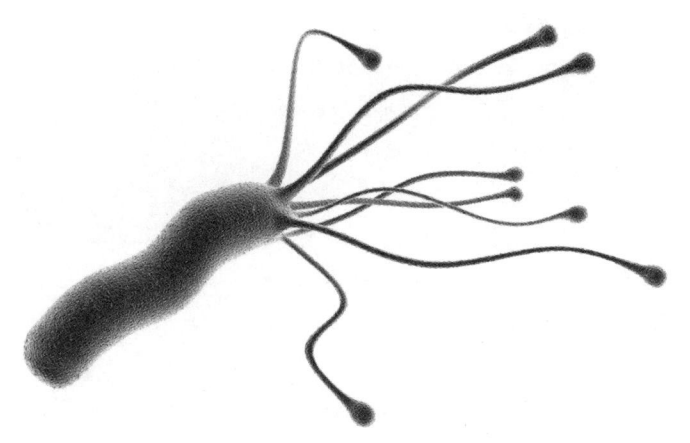

Sensing bright light might be very useful for an organism like this

its body that were just a tiny bit sensitive to light. These few cells couldn't 'see', but they could sense the difference between bright light and no light (nothing else: just bright light, or no light).

Now it's very likely that being able to tell bright light from no light gave this creature a definite **advantage** in getting food. It could tell, for example, where the sky was (bright light) and where the sky wasn't (no light). And if the organisms it fed on lived near the surface of the ocean, for example, then suddenly it would have information about where to find food ('follow the bright light') – information that the rest of the species wouldn't have.

Suddenly it would have an advantage – it would be better suited to its environment.

Over a long, long time, it is likely that creatures with these light-sensitive cells would become much more common, and the totally blind versions would become much less common.

Over squillions of generations, over hundreds of millions of years, those few light-sensitive cells might grow in size, move to a more useful place on the body (like facing forward), develop ways of distinguishing colours, and so on. Eventually it might even develop a simple kind of lens, so it could see things in a bit more detail.

Now each of these changes would give the creature an **evolutionary advantage** over its competitors, although we'd hardly call any of it 'an eye'.

Where does life come from?

How did life on planet Earth start in the first place? We know that life did not begin with the beginning of the universe, with the Big Bang. Life must have started much, much later. So how did 'life' come out of 'no life'? Where did life come from?

Simple life

No matter how life started, we can be pretty sure that it started out as something relatively simple, and then became more complex. Instead of thinking about 'life' as being the complex kinds of organisms we see around us today, we need

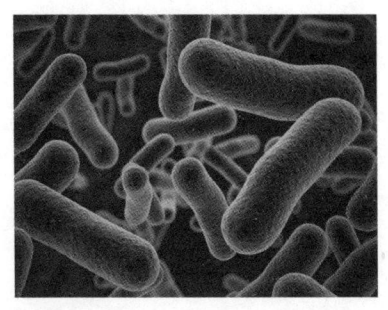

Bacteria

think of early 'life' as being tiny, simple **microorganisms** – a bit like **bacteria**.

In fact we can look at the **fossil record** here on Earth to see what kinds of organisms were living on the planet at different times in Earth's history. The earliest known life forms that we have identified in this way are tiny fossils of bacteria, called **microfossils**, dating to about 3.45 billion years ago. (Microfossils are fossils that are usually less than about one millimetre in size.) We'll look at microfossils again when we talk about how quickly life starts, later in this chapter.

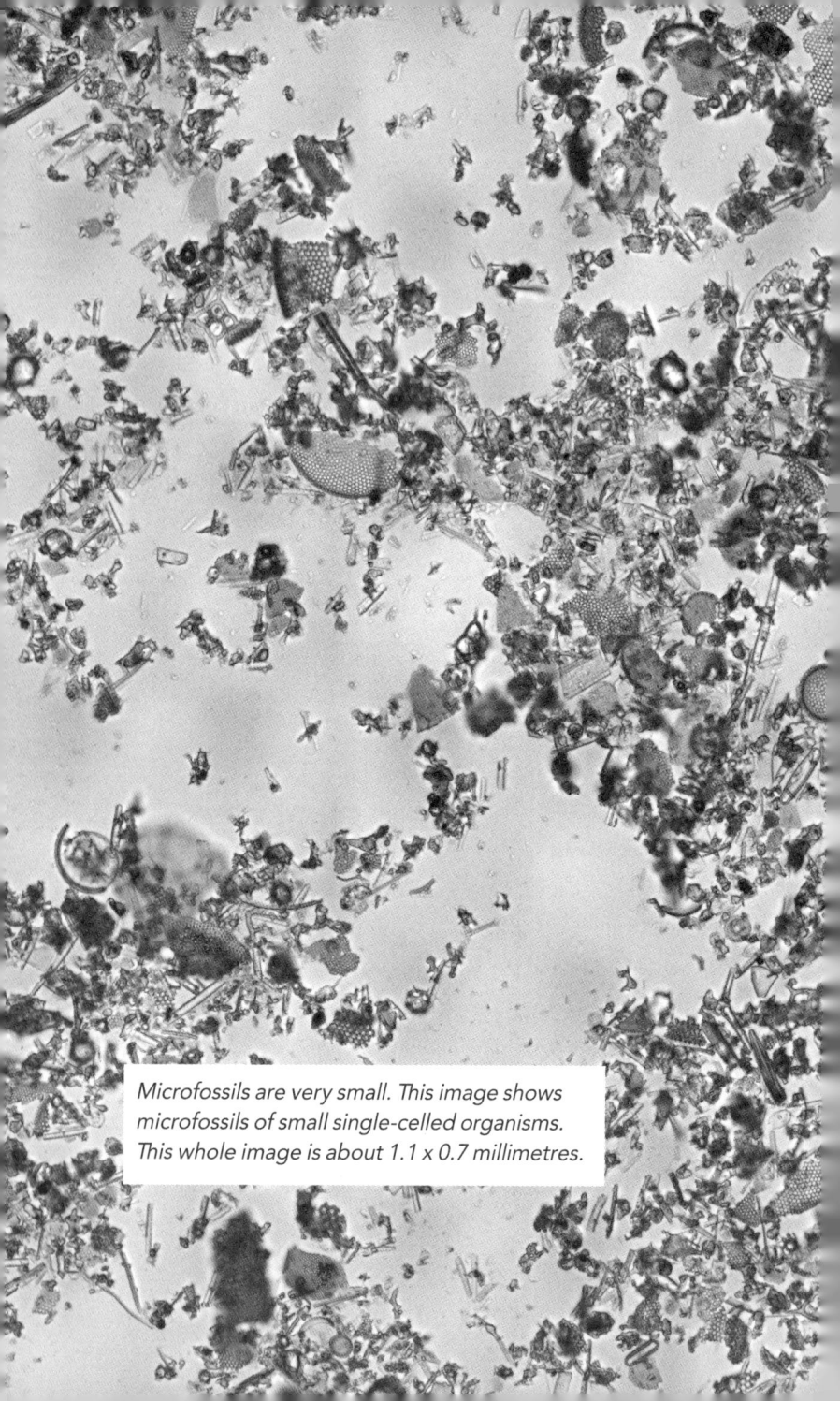

Microfossils are very small. This image shows microfossils of small single-celled organisms. This whole image is about 1.1 x 0.7 millimetres.

How did life start?

We know that life didn't start as a result of a spark of electricity striking a fully-formed 'creature' and bringing it to life. That only happens in the movies (and in horror stories), I'm afraid.

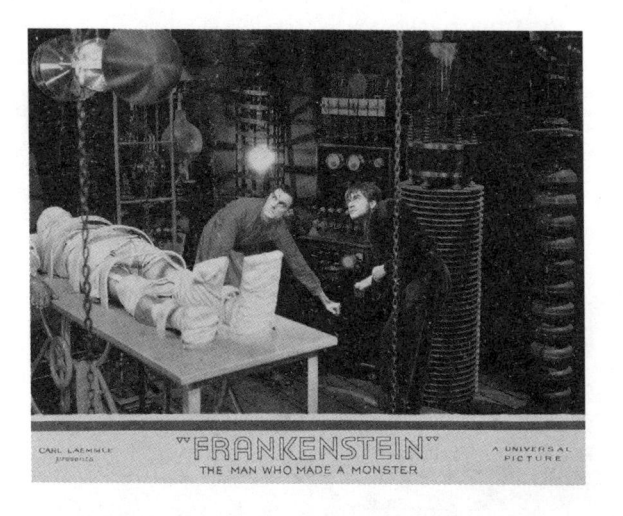

Scientists agree that the move from non-living things to living organisms wasn't a single event. Rather, it was a gradual process that probably took a very long time. We don't know exactly how life started on Earth, but scientists have suggested a number of ways that it could have happened. Here are a few of them.

Clay World

This theory was first suggested in the 1960s by the Scottish chemist Graham Cairns-Smith. Clay (the stuff we use to make pots) is a complex combination of different **elements**.

The chemistry's a bit complicated, but it's possible that the first things that could make copies of themselves (**replicators**) were simple crystals – minerals and clay. These crystals can grow, or **replicate**, if the conditions are right. (Do you remember doing any experiments growing crystals at school?)

We know that different kinds of crystals can actually be made from the same **atoms**. Graphite and diamonds, for example, are both made of exactly the same atoms (**carbon**), but one is very, very soft and the other is very, very hard. The only difference is in the *structure* of their crystals.

Graphite (the lead in pencils) and diamonds are both made of carbon atoms

It's not hard to see that if one crystal structure is better suited to the environment than another – then we have a kind of natural selection.

Molecular tool kits

This theory suggests that before there were bacteria, there were simpler, half-living things, a bit like viruses.

Now, in a way, viruses are just huge complex crystals which can do things – including make copies of themselves, with variations. The viruses that we know today need living things to live inside, but what about a different kind of 'virus' that is able to make copies of itself and that is half-way between 'not alive' chemistry and 'alive' bacteria?

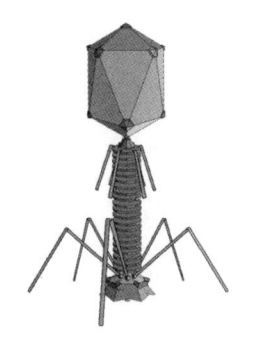

A diagram of a virus

The scientist **Manfred Eigen** has suggested that these virus-like things could have built up a 'molecular tool kit' (as he calls it) that living cells used to recreate themselves.

Perhaps these virus-like things also built around them what eventually became simple, protective cell walls: in other words, the beginnings of bodies.

Primeval Soup

In 1953, **Harold Urey**, a Nobel prize-winning chemist, worked with student **Stanley Miller** to try to recreate what Earth was like when it was very young. They carried out an experiment which has now become famous.

In their laboratories they linked two flasks with two glass tubes. They partly filled the lower flask with water (representing the Earth's oceans) and above the water they introduced the gases that they thought were in the atmosphere of the early Earth.

(These were methane, ammonia, hydrogen and water vapour.) They then heated the water and created electrical sparks inside the flasks, similar to lightning. They had recreated the early Earth in their laboratory.

After a few days of this they found they had produced a sludge of different molecules: a kind of primeval soup. Amongst these molecules were what we call **amino acids**, which we know are the building blocks of life.

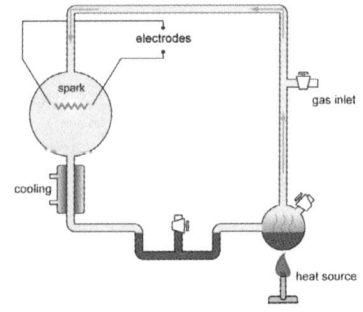

Urey and Miller's experiment

Did they create life in a test-tube? No. But they did get a few steps on the way to doing so – and they'd done it in just a few days. Evolution had many millions of years to do the same thing!

Where did life start?

How life started and *where* life started are two different questions, although they are of course related. If we don't know exactly how life started, do we have any idea where it started?

We used to think that life started in a kind of warm, muddy puddle somewhere; this idea followed from Miller and Urey's **primeval soup** experiment described above. But more recently scientists have realised that there are actually many places where life could have started.

We have already talked in Chapter Two about the theory of **panspermia** – the idea that life came to Earth from outer space. We have also talked (in the same Chapter) about the **hydrothermal vents**, deep under the oceans, where life has gained a firm hold – even though it would never have occurred to anybody that's a place where life could begin, or even survive. These deep sea vents have given scientists who are interested in the beginnings of life a lot to think about.

For example, there is a **microorganism** living on the **black smokers** called Methanococcus jannaschii. (Who names these things? Why not just call it Bob?)

This microorganism is happiest at a temperature between 50 and 90 degrees Celsius (that's not far off the boiling point of water) and at pressures that are 200 times normal air pressure. Those are conditions that would kill most other organisms.

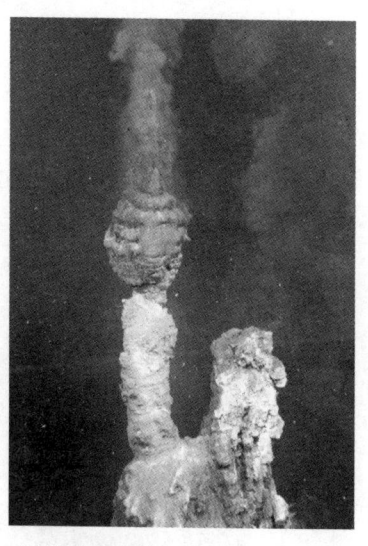

A black smoker

More interesting, oxygen is poisonous to this organism. Instead it needs carbon dioxide, nitrogen and hydrogen (the three things that spew from these deep sea vents). There aren't many places on Earth where this organism could survive, yet it's perfectly suited for living on these black smokers.

Some scientists have suggested that life on Earth may have started around these deep sea vents and then spread to other parts of the planet.

Is water essential for life?

Scientists think that water is one of the things that is essential for life. Certainly on our planet there is plenty of water (we don't call it 'the blue planet' for nothing), and as far as we know all life on

The blue planet

Earth needs water to survive. 'No water, no life,' everybody says. That's the rule.

We *think* this is true, but of course we can't be sure. All it would take is for one life form to come along that doesn't need water and we would be proved wrong straight away.

Make sure you know the difference between not needing water at all and not needing much water, though. These little creatures are called **tardigrades**, or water bears. Sometimes they're called moss piglets.

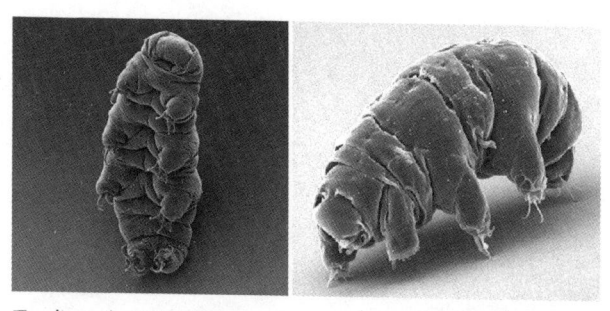

Tardigrades (also known as water bears or moss piglets)

They are very small – only about half a millimetre in length, and they have been found all over our planet: at the tops of mountains, deep under the sea, in tropical rainforests and even in the Antarctic. They seem to be able to survive almost anywhere.

They are interesting because we know that they can survive for more than 30 years without food or water.

Some tardigrades can survive in very cold temperatures (down to minus 270 degrees Celsius, which is close to **absolute zero**) and others can survive temperatures of up to 150 degrees Celsius (hotter than boiling water).

Tardigrades are also the only animals we know of that can survive in outer space. As part of an experiment, groups of tardigrades were exposed to the vacuum and radiation of outer space for ten days. After being taken back to Earth, a few were successfully revived.

These creatures have made scientists think very carefully about how tough some kinds of life can be (or could be). But we need to remember that tardigrades survive these extreme environments by shutting their bodies down and just waiting until things get better. They aren't actually **adapted** to live in such harsh conditions – they're just able to survive them.

The habitable zone

Because water is regarded as essential for life, scientists who study solar systems are very interested in what they call the **habitable zone**.

Any solar system that has planets orbiting a star, and possibly moons orbiting some of the planets, will have some planets that are closer to the star and some that are further away.

Any planets that are too close to the star will be very hot and any water on those planets will evaporate away. So life will not be able to start or survive there. On the other hand, planets that are very far away will be too cold for liquid water to exist. Again, that is no good for life.

But planets that are not too close and not too far away will have the right temperatures for liquid water to exist. This is the habitable zone. In our solar system, planet Earth is in this zone.

Our solar system showing the habitable zone (not to scale)

The habitable zone is sometimes called the **Goldilocks zone**, after the tale of Goldilocks and the three bears: everything needs to be just right, not too hot and not too cold.

Of course, when we are looking at any solar system, it is quite possible that the habitable zone (if it exists) might have no planets in it at all.

Recently scientists have had to **rethink** their ideas about the habitable zone. They used to think that this zone was the only place in a solar system where life could exist, for the reasons just explained. But scientists now realise that even planets or moons that are further away, where little heat comes from the star, might be able to support liquid water and therefore life. This is because the heat given out by the star may not be the only source of heat.

As we have already discussed (on page 25), scientists have been looking closely at Jupiter's moon **Europa** and Saturn's moon **Enceladus**.

These moons are way beyond our solar system's habitable zone, but it seems that both moons have internal sources of heat. We

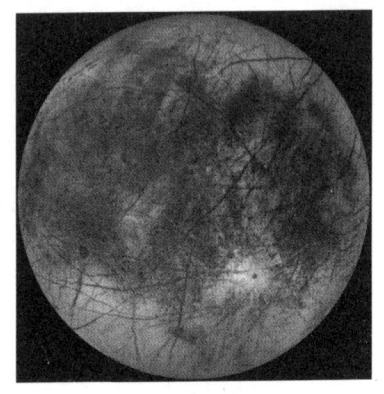

Jupiter's moon Europa

think that this heat comes from active hydrothermal vents inside the moons. These two small moons are constantly being pulled by the gravitational forces of the two huge planets they orbit, Jupiter and Saturn. It seems that these forces are squashing and stretching the moons, heating them up internally.

Certainly for Enceladus, as we discussed in Chapter Two, scientists have seen huge jets, or geysers, of liquid water leaving the moon, and in 2018 the Cassini space probe found **organic molecules**, the building blocks of life, in these jet plumes.

Scientists also think that there might even be an ocean of liquid water about 10 km deep under the surface of Enceladus.

Saturn's moon Enceladus, showing what looks like long fracture lines in the moon's surface. Photo taken by the Cassini spacecraft

So even though both moons are outside the habitable zone, we think that there could be life there.

The lesson seems to be that being in the habitable zone is one way to get liquid water for life, but it's definitely not the only way. The conditions for life can exist in places we would never have expected.

How quickly does life get going?

If the conditions are right for life, how quickly does life appear? Is it something that happens quite quickly (in **geological time**), or is it a rare event that takes a very long time to get started?

The only life we know of is the life we see on our own planet Earth, so that's the only evidence that we can look at.

We know how old these rocks are. If there are any fossils in these rocks, we'll know how old they are, too

Of course we weren't around when life first appeared on Earth, so we can only make estimates based on the evidence.

The best evidence we have is the **fossil record**. Because we can calculate the ages of Earth's rocks very accurately, it means that we can also calculate the ages of any fossils that we find in those rocks.

We think that the Earth formed about 4,540 million years ago. At that time the Earth would have been very hot, with lots of volcanic activity, and the surface of the Earth would probably have been molten. We think the oceans formed about 4,410 million years ago.

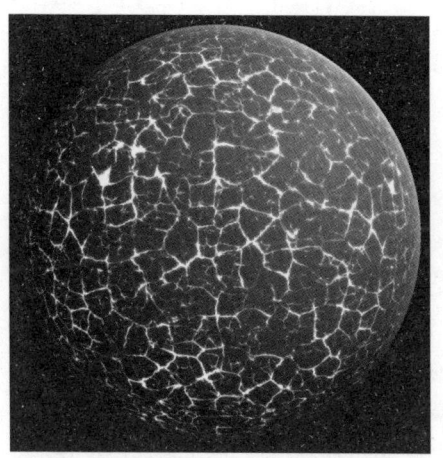

An artist's impression of the Earth during its formation, about 4.5 billion years ago

The earliest known life forms we have actually discovered in the fossil record are **microfossils** of bacteria, which we have found in what is now Australia. These microfossils are 3,450 million years old, which would mean that life started no later than about a billion years after the formation of the Earth.

There are also quite a few other fossil finds around the world that tell us that life was established on Earth by around this time.

But there is also some evidence that life began much, much earlier than this. In 2017, fossilised **microorganisms** were discovered near hydrothermal vents in Canada, and some scientists think that these fossils may be as old as 4,280 million years. If that is true, it would mean that life had already got started on Earth just 260,000 years after the Earth formed – and just 130,000 years after the oceans formed.

On the geological timescale (where everything takes a very long time), that is very, very quick! In fact it is almost instant. It suggests that, wherever the conditions for life are right, life will get going pretty much straight away. (But, I stress, we have only one planet as evidence – our own planet Earth.)

Fossils

We need to remember that these dates for when life started on Earth are based upon what scientists have seen in the fossil record.

The important thing to remember about fossils is that only the **hard parts** of organisms' bodies are preserved. Any organisms that are **soft-bodied**, that don't have hard parts such as bones or teeth, generally won't appear in the rocks as fossils. So we won't know about them.

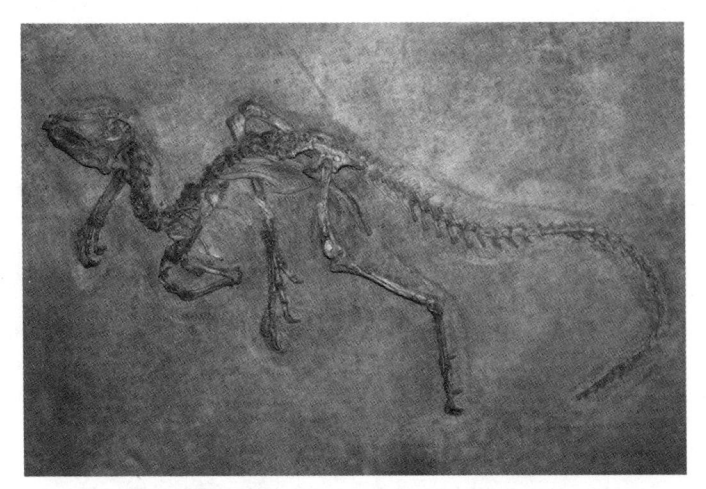

Organisms without hard body parts usually don't appear in the fossil record

So it is quite possible in fact that life started on Earth some time *before* it first appeared in the fossil record.

Timeline Earth

It can be difficult to appreciate some of the **timescales** involved when we talk about the history of the Earth. So, to put it in perspective, let's collapse the history of Earth into a single imaginary twenty-four-hour day.

Let's say that the Earth was formed at midnight at the beginning of our twenty-four-hour day, and where we are now, in the first quarter of the twenty-first century, is midnight, twenty-four hours later.

In this day, one hour is equivalent to just over 189 million years of Earth time. Just one second on our twenty-four hour clock is equivalent to 52,500 years of Earth time. Or to put it another way, the life of a single human lasts about 0.0019 seconds on our clock. Does that help to put things in perspective?

So, at what times on our twenty-four-hour clock did the important events on Earth happen? (See opposite.)

- The **oceans** formed at about 41 minutes after midnight.
- The first, **simple life** appeared at about 6 o'clock in the morning. (If life started as far back as 4,280 million years ago, as some scientists think, then that would have been at about twenty-past one in the morning – just eighty minutes after the Earth formed.)
- The first **multicellular organisms** appeared at about two-thirty in the afternoon.
- The first **life on land** appeared at about seven o'clock in the evening.
- The first **mammals** appeared at about 11.15 pm.
- **Hominids** (human-like creatures) first appeared at about two minutes to midnight.
- **Homo sapiens**? (That's us humans.) We appeared about five seconds ago!

The history of the Earth collapsed into a 24-hour day

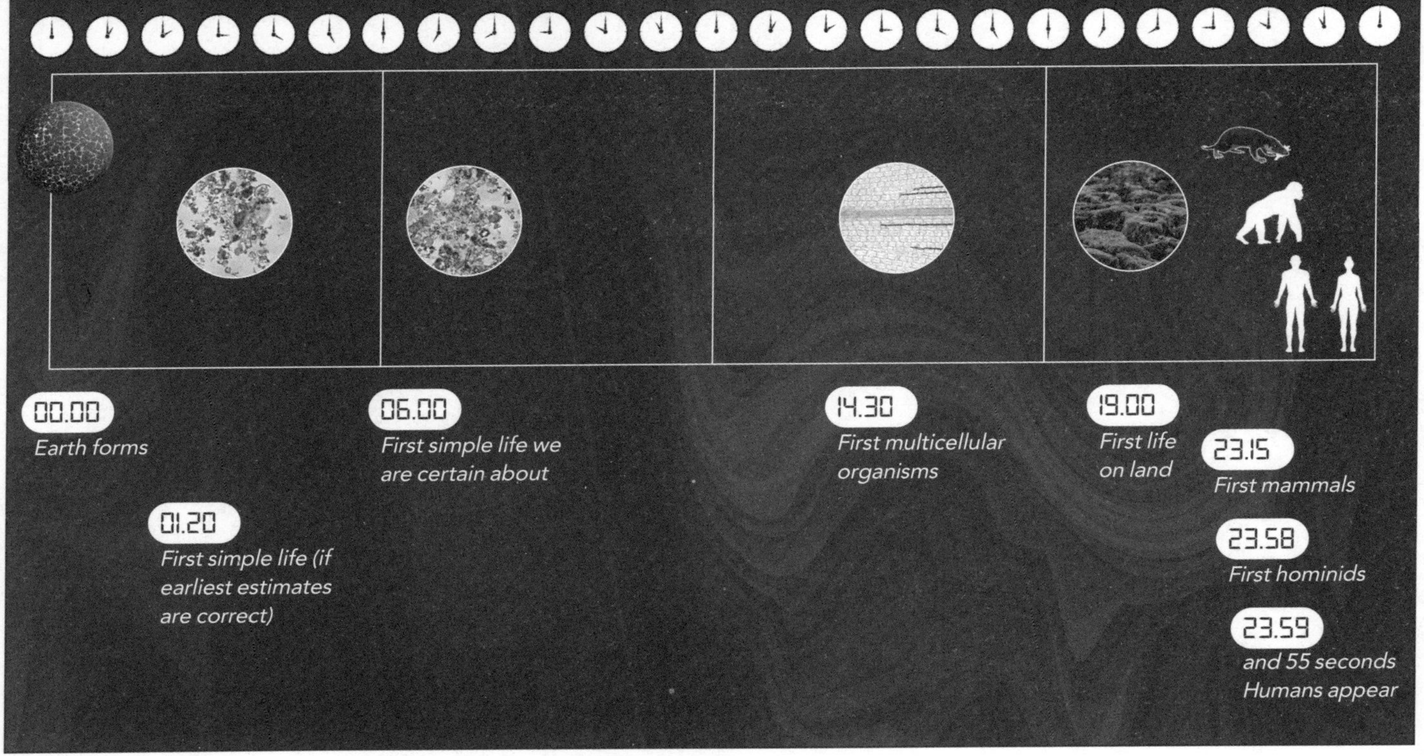

00.00 Earth forms

01.20 First simple life (if earliest estimates are correct)

06.00 First simple life we are certain about

14.30 First multicellular organisms

19.00 First life on land

23.15 First mammals

23.58 First hominids

23.59 and 55 seconds Humans appear

So for a mind-numbing two billion years, the first ten hours (or so) after it emerged, life just continued on as simple, single-celled organisms, as simple as it gets.

Life elsewhere?

What does this all mean for the chances of life elsewhere in the universe? Well, one of the most remarkable things about life on Earth is that it did appear so early. The point at which life was **theoretically** possible – about four billion years ago – was just about the point that life actually appeared.

That would suggest that, if the conditions are right, life is something that will start very, very quickly.

If that is true, the question isn't, 'How rare is life?' Rather, it is, 'How many places in the universe have the right conditions for life?' Because, it seems, if the conditions are right, life will emerge.

Intelligent life

Most life on planet Earth isn't 'intelligent'. That isn't a criticism of any kind – it's a simple statement of fact.

If we look at life on planet Earth, it's clear that we humans have 'jumped ahead' of other species on the planet. We have pretty much taken over the planet:

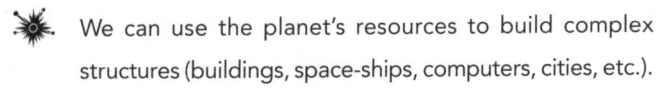

- We can use complex language (and we can write it down and then let others read it).
- We can use the planet's resources to build complex structures (buildings, space-ships, computers, cities, etc.).

Signs of human activity are everywhere on Earth. We have built complex structures and interconnected cities

- We can investigate the world around us.
- We can harness electricity and nuclear power.
- We are aware of ourselves. We have **consciousness**; we can think about ourselves and we can think about thinking.

We human beings do think of ourselves as being 'intelligent life' – and we do think that we are the only species on planet Earth that falls into this category.

For example, we all assume that if aliens do one day contact our planet, it's us humans that they'll want to make contact with. But can we be sure of that? What if they came to make contact with **dolphins**, for example? We know that dolphins are in fact very intelligent. What if aliens have made contact with dolphins already?

How intelligent are dolphins? It certainly looks as though they are much more intelligent than we used to think. For example,

Dolphins are highly intelligent species

hominids – including ourselves – have super-long spindle **neurons** in parts of their brains. We know that these cells have something to do with our **social behaviour**, with our **emotions** and **judgement**, and with our awareness of ourselves.

Well, in 2007 scientists found these kinds of spindle cells in the brains of some dolphins. In fact, some scientists think that dolphins are **self-aware**, just as we are.

By the way, a few paragraphs back I said this about intelligent life:

it's clear that we humans have 'jumped ahead' of other species on the planet.

I hope you flinched when you read the words 'jumped ahead' as much as I did when I wrote them. It makes it sound as if there is some kind of **evolutionary ladder** that all species on Earth are busy climbing up, and we humans are nearest the top, being followed by all the other species on the planet.

No. No. No. No. No. It's an easy trap to fall into, but it's wrong. There is no 'ladder' and there is no race. Different species become adapted to the different environments that they live in, and well-adapted species are the ones that survive.

We would do as badly in their environments as they would in ours. We could never be as successful as dolphins are in their environment, just as we could never live on the black smokers which the microorganisms Methanococcus jannaschii (earlier in this chapter) happily call their home.

We can use what we know about how life developed on planet Earth to guess how life might develop elsewhere in the universe. The stages might be:

1. Life begins with simple **replicators**.
2. Over a very long period of time, life becomes more complex, leading to single-celled organisms, multicellular creatures and eventually a huge variety of complex organisms living alongside each other.
3. Possibly at some point one species (could it be more than one?) takes a huge leap 'forward' and becomes what we would call **intelligent**.
4. This species would probably dominate the planet (or moon, or wherever they are living). This species would develop advanced technology and, like us, start thinking about life in other parts of the universe …

(I'm trying to keep this really simple; otherwise we get into a huge debate about intelligent life and what makes up intelligence. That's really a whole book in itself!)

So … is that how it works?

Well, on planet Earth 'non-intelligent' life has been around a lot longer than 'intelligent' life. Looking at the diagram in this chapter collapsing the history of the Earth into a twenty-four-hour day, intelligent life did not appear until the last two minutes or so of our day. That is very late.

Is this a **typical** pattern? Could intelligent life emerge much, much sooner? To be honest, we simply don't know.

A narrow window?

I should mention one other thing here. When an intelligent species appeared on Earth (ourselves, we humans), it led to huge technology changes that improved our lives massively. Most of us have safe drinking water and heated homes, we have medicines and we can all expect to live for a long time. But these changes have also brought with them the power to destroy the whole planet.

We have polluted our planet so badly that we are killing off other species at a terrifying rate.

- We have produced (and we now store) enough **nuclear weapons** to destroy our entire planet many times over.
- We use nuclear energy with no thought about what will happen to the **nuclear waste** we create. It will remain dangerous for tens, if not hundreds, of thousands of years.
- We build nuclear power plants that are not always safe.
- We are the main cause of **global warming**.
- We risk making our planet **uninhabitable**: we risk making it impossible for us and for all other species to live on it.

On Earth, we have caused a lot of **damage** to our planet and we have not yet developed technology to travel to distant stars. It is possible that in some cases, when intelligent life emerges on a planet, it is not able to survive long enough to reach the stage where it is advanced enough to travel through interstellar space.

Perhaps there is a pattern: intelligent life emerges, it creates planet-changing technologies – and then it destroys itself, or destroys its planet, or both, in quite a short time, before it has learned how to behave responsibly.

In the 1951 film *The Day the Earth Stood Still*, an alien called Klaatu travels to Earth with a message. He explains that the people of other planets have seen humans developing weapons and nuclear power, and they are worried by the warlike attitude of the human race. This threatens the safety of all planets.

So Klaatu tells the people of Earth that they have a choice: they can learn to live in peace with the peoples of other planets, or they can carry on as they are. But if humans don't change, says Klaatu, then for the safety of the rest of the universe, the human race will be destroyed.

What will aliens look like?

If we ever meet alien life, what will it look like? Will aliens look like the creatures we see on TV and in the movies? Will they look like us? Or could they look like something completely unexpected? Could we be in for a big surprise?

Well since we haven't encountered alien life, we can't say for

What will aliens look like?

sure what it will look like. But there are some things about our aliens that we can probably say with some confidence.

Seven criteria

First of all, since our aliens will be (by definition) alive, we can say that they will probably meet our seven criteria for life.

The Seven Criteria for Life
1 Reproduction
2 Growth
3 Nutrition
4 Respiration
5 Excretion
6 Senses
7 Locomotion

So they will be able to reproduce, grow, feed, breathe, get rid of waste products, sense the world around them in some way, and move around their world.

Standard design solutions

If our seven criteria for life are correct, then both alien life and life on Earth will need to do the same kinds of things. They will need to feed, move around, sense the world around them, and so on.

Now there's probably a limit to the number of ways that some of these things can be done. And if we look at the variety of life on Earth, we will see that a lot of the best **design solutions**, the best ways of getting these things done, are already being used.

A few ways of moving around on Earth

Take **moving around**, for example. If you think of all the organisms on Earth that move around, how many different ways of moving can you think of? Here are a few.

- Walking on two legs
- Walking on four or more legs
- Hopping
- Slithering
- 'Swimming' (in water)
- Flying

Can you think of any good ways of moving around that aren't on the above list?

Evolution is a great way of finding good design solutions to tricky problems. So maybe any solutions not already found on Earth just aren't good solutions.

Like using **wheels**, instead of legs, to move around. Wheels sound like a great idea – after all, our cars, trains, bicycles and so on all use wheels. So why not aliens with wheels instead of legs?

Well it turns out that wheels aren't a great solution after all.

The wheel is not a good design solution for living things

The problem is that wheels **rotate**, and they need to rotate around something – an axle. So there's immediately a problem with **friction**. How do you stop your bits wearing away where the wheel meets the axle and rubs against it every time it moves?

After all, cars don't usually last more than 10 or 15 ye[ars]
that wear out can always be replaced. Our bodies
every minute of every day for decades, without wea[r]

And how do you get up steps or climb ladders if you have wheels?

So actually, aliens are probably going to have found the same kinds of design solutions to the basic problems of living that creatures on Earth have already found. Unless, of course, their home planet's environment gives them completely different kinds of problems to solve.

How big will they be?

How big will our aliens be? Scientists know that on Earth it's sometimes best to be big and sometimes best to be small.

How big will they be?

Dinosaurs were huge, and they dominated the planet (OK, until they were all wiped out, I admit). But sometimes it's better to be small, so you don't get noticed. It's all about finding the best way to survive in your environment.

There is one important factor that does affect the size (and especially the shape) of an organism, and that is **gravity**. Assuming that gravity will exist on our aliens' world (we are sure that gravity is a universal law), then the aliens will need to be strong enough to support the weight of their bodies.

If the force of gravity on their planet is greater than it is on Earth, they'd need stronger bodies to support themselves than they would here on Earth.

Early science-fiction films often showed aliens from Mars as being tall, slender creatures. This is because we know that gravity on the planet Mars is not as strong as on Earth, so the aliens wouldn't need such powerful bodies to support themselves. (Although if those Martians ever came here, Earth's gravity might cause them some problems.)

Aliens from low-gravity planets might look long and spindly to us.

In this chapter we have looked at what **life** is and how the process of **natural selection** explains how life changes over time. We have looked at how and where life might have started on Earth, and explored how quickly life might get started once the conditions are right. We also looked briefly at what **alien life** might be like, if we were ever to meet it.

Now it is time to bring together our understanding of the history of the universe with our understanding of life, to focus on the chances of our really meeting aliens.

And we will do that next.

" The only reason for time is so that everything doesn't happen at once. "

Albert Einstein

WRONG PLACE, WRONG TIME

In Chapters Three and Four we explored the **universe** that we live in (well, not literally!) and concluded that it is a very big place indeed. We discovered that some parts of the universe are so far away from each other that it isn't possible to travel from the one part to the other, or even to send messages across such vast distances. We also looked at how long the universe has been around, and how it has been changing over time (and will continue to change).

In Chapter Five we looked at **life**: how it might have started, the conditions necessary for life to exist and how life changes over time. We also looked at how quickly life got started on Earth, and how long it took for intelligent life to emerge.

Now we can put all of these findings together to try to give a better answer to our question, 'Why haven't we seen aliens?'

To keep things (relatively) simple, I am going to make some **assumptions**.

- I am going to assume that alien life does in fact exist elsewhere in the universe.

- I am going to assume that this alien life is intelligent. In fact, I am going to assume that our aliens are more advanced than our human civilisation on Earth, and that they have already developed space-ships that are capable of travelling across **interstellar space**. In other words, they have space-ships that can travel beyond their own solar system to other star systems.

- I am also going to assume that this alien life is **curious** to find out whether there is life elsewhere in the universe. Of course these aliens might already have met other alien civilisations, but I think that would not stop them continuing to look. In fact, I think it would probably encourage them.

I am assuming that our aliens will be able to travel to other star systems

> ☀ I am also going to assume that these aliens do not intend to destroy us as soon as they find out that we exist. (This is a tricky topic and we'll come back to it in the next chapter.)

So. What are the chances?

Well, if aliens are going to arrive here, they will need to be in the right **place** (planet Earth) and at the right **time** (kind of 'now' – when we are here). That's the only way we'll get to meet them (at least until we start travelling to other planets ourselves).

Let's look at each of these in turn.

Wrong place?

The universe is big. Very big. It is so big that we cannot see or know anything about parts of it.

As you will no doubt remember, this is because some parts of the universe are so far away that light travelling from there to here, to us on Earth, will take longer to reach us than the entire time the universe has been in existence.

In other words, to reach us now, that light would have to have set out more than 13.8 billion years ago, which is the time when we think the Big Bang happened, when the universe began. And since we don't think there was anything before the Big Bang, that is impossible.

So those parts of the universe are completely closed off to us. Any light (or messages, not to mention space-ships) from those parts to Earth haven't had enough time to reach us.

So if any aliens are in those parts, they won't be able to communicate with us at all (and we won't be able to communicate with them).

To make things more difficult, we think that the universe is **expanding** at high speed. So, as time passes, these **unobservable** parts of the universe are moving away from us very quickly. So the chances of our communicating with these parts of the universe are getting less likely as time goes on.

The galaxy cluster MACS J1149.5+2223, photographed by the Hubble Space Telescope.

The inset image (in the white rectangle) is the galaxy MACS1149-JD1, seen as it was 13.3 billion years ago – just half a billion years after the Big Bang

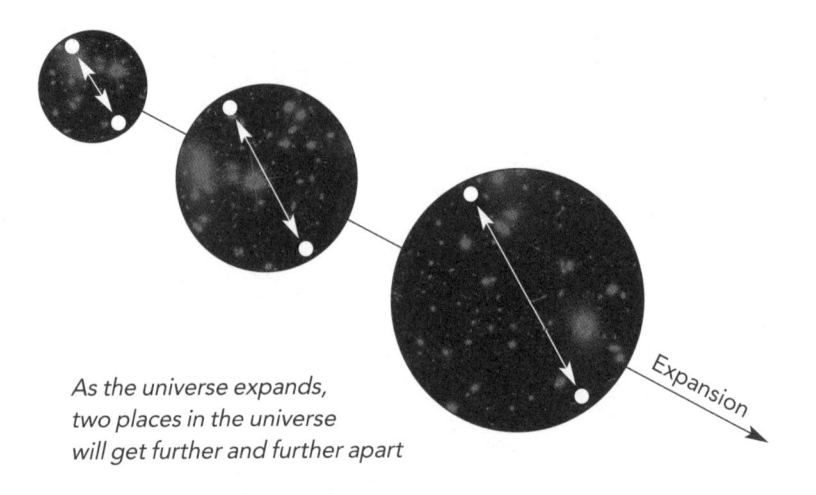

As the universe expands, two places in the universe will get further and further apart

Expansion →

So if we ignore those very distant parts of the universe, what's left is the **observable universe**, the part of the universe that, **theoretically** at least, we should be able to see. What can we say about that? Here's a quick summary of what we discovered in Chapters Three and Four:

- We think the observable universe is about **93 billion light-years** in diameter. That means that from Earth we can 'see' the universe around us for about 46 billion light-years in any direction. 
- We think there are between about 200 billion and two trillion galaxies in the universe. Each galaxy has between about a hundred million and a

hundred trillion stars in it (needless to say, again, these are just estimates).

- That would put the number of stars in the universe at between **20 quintillion** and **200 septillion** (that's 2 followed by 26 zeros). That is a *lot* of stars.

- Not all stars will have planets and some stars will have many planets.

- We're pretty sure that life won't be found on stars. If we are going to find life, it will probably be found on planets or moons orbiting planets.

Alien life is most likely to be found on an exoplanet or exomoon

- So any way you look at it, there seems to be a lot of places where life might have the **opportunity** to get started.

Now, assuming that all the **stars** and **galaxies** in the observable universe are evenly spread out (they aren't, but let's keep it simple), how many stars are close enough to our planet Earth for aliens to be able to visit us?

To answer that question, I need to make some more **assumptions**. Big assumptions. And I'm going to cheat here: I'm going to give our aliens the benefit of the doubt. I'm going to make assumptions that make it more likely that aliens are able to visit us.

I'm going to assume that this alien life started out very early and became **intelligent** very quickly (giving them more time to search the universe/travel to Earth), and I'm going to assume that they have very fast space-ships (which means that they can travel further in a fixed time).

So let's spell out my assumptions.

- I have assumed that the alien life we are talking about started on a planet or a moon, somewhere within range of Earth.

- I have assumed that the alien planet/moon formed, *and* life started *and* that life reached the stage we are calling 'intelligent life' – all just seven billion years after the Big Bang.

The Big Bang was 13.8 billion years ago, so I'm assuming that this intelligent alien life appeared say 6.8 billion years ago. This is life that is intelligent enough to

Will intelligent aliens live in cities?

design and build a space-ship that could travel extremely quickly.

Just for comparison – the Earth formed about 4.5 billion years ago, which is about 9.3 billion years after the Big Bang. And intelligent life appeared on Earth so recently that, on the **timescales** we are talking about, we might as well call it 'now'. Which is say 4.5 billion years after the Earth formed and about 13.8 billion years after the Big Bang.

So I've given alien intelligent life a 6.8 billion year head start over ourselves on planet Earth.

This table sums up how much faster than here on Earth I've assumed that our alien life would develop:

	Alien planet	**Earth**
Big Bang	13.8 bya*	13.8 bya
Planet formed	?	4.5 bya
Life started	?	3.5 bya
Intelligent life	6.8 bya	'now'
(* All figures are billion years ago.)		

☀ I have also assumed that our aliens have worked out how to travel in their space-ships at very high speed — let's say at half the speed of light. So they can travel a light-year of distance in two years of time. (We don't understand how they'd be able to travel anywhere near that fast, but hey!)

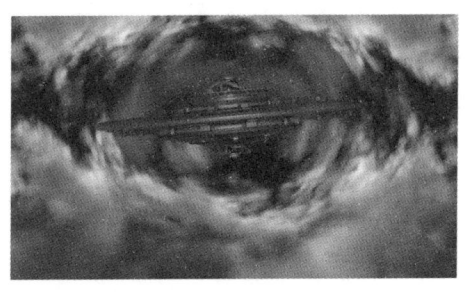

We have no idea how aliens might be able to travel at close to light speed

The observable universe, showing what I call the contact zone

So we are giving our aliens a big head start: half-light speed travel, plus a really, really early start (intelligent life appearing 6.8 billion years earlier than it did on Earth).

The large circle in the diagram above represents the observable universe, as seen from Earth: it's 46 billion light-years in any direction. Earth is in the centre of the circle (the little black dot); Earth is not shown to scale!

Now, the smaller white circle represents that part of the **observable universe** from where aliens could travel to planet Earth, based on the assumptions I've listed above. I'm calling this the **contact zone**.

How big is this contact zone? What distance could our aliens cover, travelling for 6.8 billion years at half the speed of light? The answer is that they could travel about 3.4 billion light-years. Which is roughly the size of the white circle on the diagram.

In other words, any alien life within that white circle could travel to Earth – the dot in the middle – and it wouldn't take them longer than 6.8 billion years to get here. (Getting from one side of the white circle to the other side, though, a distance of 6.8 billion light years, would take (6.8 x 2 = 13.6) around 13.6 billion years. Which is very nearly the time that the universe has been in existence.

Now, trust me (or you can do the maths yourself if you want to) – the white circle on the diagram makes up just over half a percent (0.53%), or one two-hundredth, of the size of the observable universe.

So we are saying that the only aliens that could visit us (if they exist and if my assumptions above are correct) are those that are living in that 0.53% of the universe that is close enough to us.

That is a **tiny fraction** of the observable universe.

Putting it another way: any aliens elsewhere in the observable universe (that is, in the remaining 99.5%) who'd like to visit us won't be able to, because it's too far away.

And that's assuming that our alien life can travel at half the speed of light. If they aren't that quick, then the contact zone (that white circle) gets a lot, lot smaller.

Of course we're talking here just about the observable universe. If our aliens are living somewhere beyond the observable universe, well … forget it: we'll never be able to get in touch with each other.

By the way: the fastest human-built spaceship is the **Parker Solar Probe**, which reached 375,000 kilometres per hour shortly after it was launched in 2018. It's on a mission to travel very close to the Sun (where the pull of gravity is very high, which explains the high speed).

Illustration of the Parker Solar Probe approaching the Sun

By 2024 this probe is expected to reach speeds of about 680,000 kilometres per hour. Which, to put things in perspective, is still only about 0.06% of the speed of light.

So looking at just the issue of **place** – *where* they are – our aliens need to be in the one two-hundredth of the universe that is nearest to us, in order just to have a chance of meeting us. And they need super-fast spaceships.

And, at risk of stating the obvious, they need to send their space-ships out, aimed at Earth. If they sent them to the next solar system to ours, or even to say the planet Jupiter in our own solar system, we won't see them and they won't see us.

Is this how aliens would search for life?

There are a lot of other things we could talk about here. How would aliens go about exploring the universe, looking for life?

Would they launch lots of space-ships in all directions, in the hope that one of them encounters life, on the off-chance? Would they bother sending out space-ships anyway? Perhaps they might just send different kinds of messages. We'll talk about messages in the next chapter.

Wrong time?

Let's forget for a moment about *where* these aliens are in the universe. Let's assume that they're close enough to us to be able to visit us; in other words, the kinds of distances we've just talked about aren't a problem.

Let's now look at the issue of timing. Our alien explorers might set out to visit planet Earth and they might arrive here, with welcome messages at the ready. What could they find here? Well, it all depends on when they arrive. They might find …

🚀 … a planet without life. A dead planet.

A dead planet? The surface of the planet Mars, photographed by the Spirit Rover in 2004

🚀 ... a planet with **primitive life** (maybe bacteria, single-celled organisms, but nothing more).

🚀 ... a planet with **complex life**, but none that is 'intelligent'.

🚀 ... a planet with intelligent life on it, ready and willing to talk to them.

What will they find?

What are the chances of each of these happening?

Well, the Earth formed 4.5 billion years ago, so we can assume that they'll turn up some time after that. There's no point travelling to a non-existent planet to look for signs of life!

Life started on Earth roughly 3.5 billion years ago, so if our aliens had arrived in the first 700 million years after the Earth formed, they would have met a lifeless planet. No life, no us. Nothing.

Complex, multicellular life appeared on Earth about 600

million years ago. So if they'd arrived between 700 and 3,900 million years after the Earth formed, they would have met more complex life, but nothing that was 'intelligent'. Certainly not us.

In fact, in order to meet intelligent life on Earth, the aliens would have needed to arrived in the last 40,000 years or so. Or, to express it in terms of our 24-hour clock, they would have needed to turn up in the last five seconds of the 24-hour day.

So it's perfectly possible that aliens have come to visit Earth many times in the past – but each time they came, there wasn't any intelligent life here to say, 'Hello' to them.

4 billion years ago

3 billion years ago

2 billion years ago

1 billion years ago

1 million years ago

2,000 years ago

Is this how it could have happened on Earth?

We humans have been on planet Earth for a tiny, tiny fraction of the time that Earth has been around. So if aliens turned up any time in the 99.99% of the time when we weren't around, they would have missed us.

So that's why we haven't seen aliens

So the chances of aliens visiting planet Earth while we have been here are very, very remote. These aliens would need to be living in the one two-hundredth part of the universe where contact with us would be possible, and they'd have to arrive in the tiny fraction of the Earth's history when we would be here. (Basically that means the last five seconds of Earth's twenty-four-hour 'day'.)

And remember, I've assumed that our aliens can travel at half the speed of light *and* that they'd be happy to spend six billion years in a spaceship travelling to our planet. Let's face it, neither of those assumptions are very likely.

If life doesn't exist elsewhere in the universe, that would obviously explain why we haven't seen aliens. Equally, if life elsewhere in the universe is pretty rare, or not at all common, then again we shouldn't be at all surprised that we haven't seen any sign of aliens.

But if life is common throughout the universe, then the chances of there being alien life 'near' us are much higher. In that case, we can really start keeping an eye open for aliens, since they are much more likely to visit us.

Of course, if we knew how common life was in the universe, then we'd be in a much better position to work out the chances of our seeing aliens. But that's the one thing we don't have much of a clue about!

Beyond our own solar system, the nearest star to us is a small star called **Proxima Centauri**. That star is 4.25 light-years from us, and if we don't count our own solar system, then that's probably the nearest place where alien life might be lurking. (Do aliens lurk?)

*The red dwarf star Proxima Centauri.
Photograph taken by the Hubble telescope*

In fact scientists have even discovered an exoplanet orbiting Proxima Centauri. This exoplanet is called **Proxima Centauri b** (not a very original name, I know) and it's about 1.3 times bigger than Earth. Much more interesting though, scientists think that Proxima b is in the solar system's **habitable zone**. If that's true, it means that liquid water might exist on its surface. And as we've already discussed, we think that water is necessary for life.

One problem with this is that the star Proxima Centauri is quite dim – it's a type of star called a **red dwarf**. Scientists aren't sure if a red dwarf star is able to support life in its solar system, even if there is an exoplanet in the habitable zone.

Looking back in time

When we look at distant objects in the universe, we are not seeing them as they are now. Rather, we are seeing these objects as they were when the light that we are seeing them with left those objects.

So, for example, the photograph of the galaxy MACS1149-JD1 on page 145 does not show the galaxy as it is now (or, to be strictly correct, as it was when the Hubble telescope photographed it). No. The photograph shows the galaxy as it was 13.3 billion years ago. The light has taken 13.3 billion years to reach us (or rather, to reach the lens of the Hubble telescope's camera).

Even light from our own star, the Sun, takes time to reach our planet Earth. Let's try a little **thought experiment**. Imagine that you are standing on the surface of the Sun (impossible, I know) and you have a very, very bright torch that we can see from Earth (again, impossible, I know).

I'm standing on Earth, looking at the Sun. (Don't *ever* do this – the Sun will blind you. But it's OK to do it in thought experiments.) Our watches are **synchronised** – they both say exactly the same time.

Let's assume that at exactly twelve o'clock you switch the torch on for five seconds, and then switch it off again.

If I am standing somewhere on Earth, looking at the Sun and waiting for your signal, at what time would I see the torch flash? At 12.00? No. It would be at twenty seconds past 12.08 – just over eight minutes later. This is because light takes about eight minutes and twenty seconds to travel from the Sun to Earth.

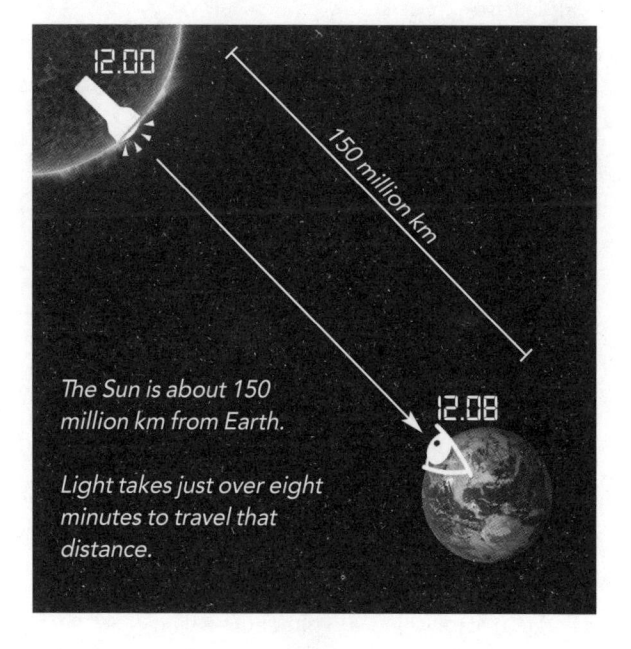

The Sun is about 150 million km from Earth.

Light takes just over eight minutes to travel that distance.

So even when you look at the Sun (or the Moon, or distant stars, or – *get this* – anything that is not right next to you), you are seeing it not as it is now, but as it was *then*, when the light left the object.

So although we live in the present, we are in fact seeing everything around us as it was in the past. *Everything.* Even the light from this book you are reading, or from the picture on the wall opposite you (if there is one), takes time to reach you (a very, very, very short time, admittedly, but it still takes time).

If you think about it, you'll realise that you're not just seeing things as they were in the past, in one single past: you're seeing things as they were in lots of different pasts, depending on how far away from you the thing you're looking at is.

I find that astonishing and rather unsettling.

Is time travel possible?

So far, all our discussions in this book have assumed that nothing can travel faster than light. (The speed of light, you may remember, is about 300,000 km per second.) Scientists think that nothing can travel faster than light – not because we haven't got the technology to do so (which we haven't anyway), but because the laws of physics say it's impossible.

But what if it *was* possible to travel faster than light?

What if we could travel faster than light?

Let's look again at the **thought experiment** we've just carried out, where somebody stands on the Sun with a torch and switches it on for five seconds at exactly twelve o'clock.

We said that, to an observer on Earth, the torch would appear to flash at eight minutes and twenty seconds past twelve, since the light takes just over eight minutes to reach Earth.

Now let's change the experiment slightly. Let's assume that the person on the Sun has a paint-ball gun as well as a torch. The torch is the same one as before, but the paint-ball gun is a special one that can fire paint balls at twice the speed of light. (I know, but it is a thought experiment!)

Let's say that at exactly 11.55 and 50 seconds (that is, four minutes and ten seconds before twelve), this person flashes their torch for five seconds, as before. (It will be clear in a moment why I chose this rather odd time to flash the torch.)

Then, four minutes and ten seconds later, at twelve o'clock exactly, this person fires one paint ball directly at the observer on Earth. The paint ball, remember, will be travelling at twice the speed of light. (We're going to ignore things like **friction** and so on, to keep things simple.)

Now, what will the observer on Earth see?

What will the person on planet Earth see?

Well, the flash of the torch was at four minutes and ten seconds before twelve. This light takes eight minutes and twenty seconds to reach the observer (it's travelling at the speed of light), so she will see the flash at four minutes and ten seconds past twelve.

What about the paint ball? That was fired at twelve o'clock exactly, but it is travelling to Earth at twice the speed of light. So its journey to the observer on Earth will take four minutes and ten seconds (half the time that the light beam takes).

So the paint ball will hit the observer at exactly four minutes and ten seconds past twelve – which is exactly the same time that the observer will see the torch flash.

The paint ball is fired after the torch is flashed, but it arrives on Earth at the same time as the flash of light.

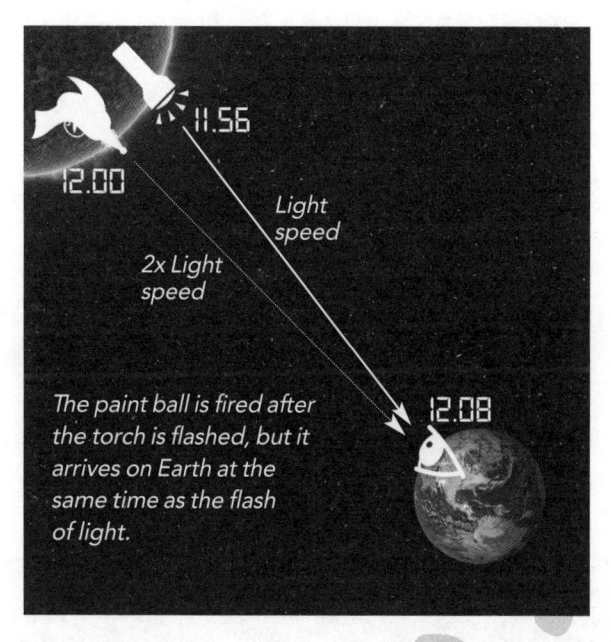

So the observer on Earth will see the torch flash and will be hit by the paint ball at exactly the same time, even though the paint ball was fired after the torch was switched on.

To the observer, the paint ball will seem to have gone back

in time; she will think it was fired at the same time that the torch was switched on, but of course it was fired later.

So, clearly, one way to go back in time, or rather to cheat time, is to travel faster than light.

If a space-ship could travel at many, many times the speed of light, it would be able to cheat time on a much larger scale. For example the nearest star to us, not counting the Sun, is the star **Proxima Centauri**, which is 4.25 light-years away. If we had a space-ship that could travel at one million times the speed of light (yes, I know!), then we could travel to that star in less than two and a half minutes!

Now all we need to do is work out how to travel at that kind of speed!

Wormholes

One way of travelling through time that scientists are looking at is using **wormholes**.

You will remember from Chapter Four that Einstein said that **space-time** is like a rubber sheet, and objects such as the Earth distort space-time by curving the rubber sheet.

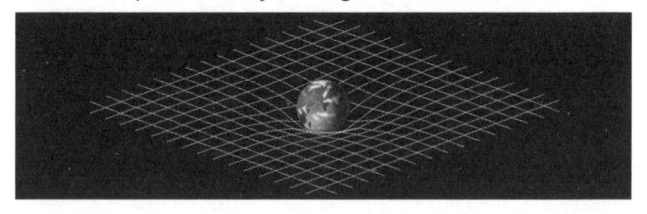

Space-time is curved by heavy objects like our planet Earth

The idea of a wormhole is that if the rubber sheet of space-time wasn't just curved a bit, but instead was actually folded back on itself (see the illustration below), then it might be possible somehow to create a **tunnel** from one point on the rubber sheet through to a second point on the same sheet.

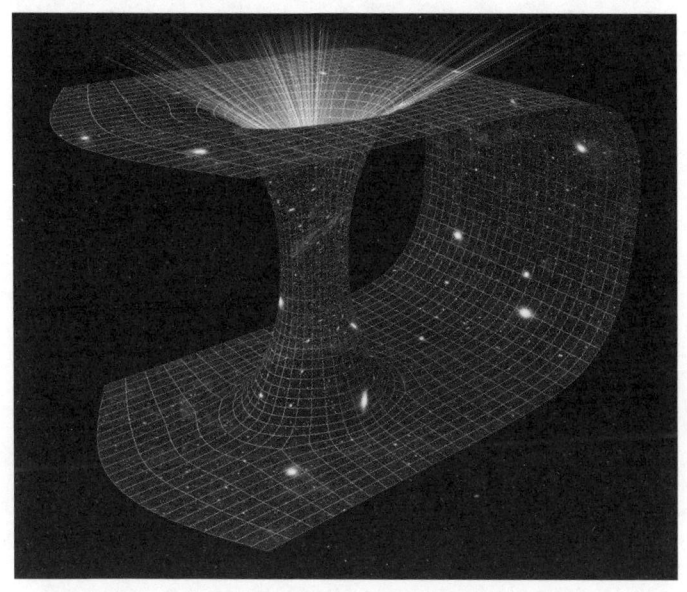

A wormhole would be a shortcut through space and time

Each end of this tunnel, or wormhole, would be at a separate point in space-time. So instead of travelling all the way around the surface of the sheet to get from the one point to the other, a traveller could simply move through the wormhole to appear in a different part of the universe much more quickly.

If the wormhole connected two points that were say billions of light years apart in the 'real' world, then this would be great way of travelling through time.

*An artist's impression of wormhole travel.
Image produced by NASA*

Do wormholes exist? Scientists say that Einstein's **theory of relativity** seems to allow them to exist, but so far nobody has discovered one or been able to create one. Certainly nobody really knows how they would work in practice, even if they do exist.

LOOKING FOR ALIENS

Rather than just sitting around waiting for aliens to visit us, we could always try looking for them ourselves.

Well, guess what? That's what some people have been doing.

SETI

SETI (the **S**earch for **E**xtra**T**errestrial **I**ntelligence) is the name given to all the scientific work being done on Earth to search for alien life.

Scientists realised quite quickly that, although aliens might visit Earth, it was much more likely that they would send out **messages** for other life forms such as ourselves to receive.

These messages could be sent in the form of visual information (**light**) or as **radio waves**.

The big advantage of sending out light or radio messages, rather than actually travelling somewhere, is that these messages can travel at the speed of light, so they can go much further and much more quickly than boring old space-ships.

The other advantage of course is that you don't have to bother building a boring old space-ship and you don't have to work out how to survive very long, boring journeys in space.

There are lots of things to see out in space, so lots of light waves are continually heading our way. Plus, radio waves of all kinds are constantly bombarding our planet Earth. So the big problem for SETI scientists is how to work out what, out of all this jumble of information, might really be a message from an alien civilisation.

Radio waves travel in all directions. Laser beams travel in one direction only

If light is going to be used to send a message, then that light would need to be very powerful to travel long distances. That means that **laser beams** would probably need to be used to create such powerful light.

The problem with lasers is that they are highly **directional**, which means that you can only see the light message if it is pointing towards you. A radio message, on the other hand, travels in all directions, covering much more of the universe. For this reason scientists have decided that aliens are more likely to send a radio message than a light message, so they have spent more time *listening* for radio messages than *looking* at the sky for a light message.

Scientists use **radio telescopes** to search for radio

A radio telescope: the VLA (Very Large Array) in New Mexico, USA

messages. A radio telescope is a bit like an ordinary telescope, except that it magnifies radio waves rather than light waves.

Over the past 100 years or so many scientists around the world have been listening out for something that might be a message from aliens. But so far they haven't seen or heard anything that is *definitely* from an alien civilisation. There have been a few false alarms, though.

False alarms

In 1967 a young scientist, **Jocelyn Bell Burnell**, was working in astronomy (nothing to do with SETI) when she discovered a very strong **radio pulse** coming from somewhere out in space. The pulse was very strong and happened about every 1.3 seconds.

Nobody knew what it was, so first thoughts were that it might be a message from aliens. In fact at first it was given the name **LGM-1**, which stood for 'Little Green Men 1'.

In fact it wasn't a message from aliens at all; Jocelyn Bell Burnell had discovered a **pulsar**, something we knew nothing about at the time. A

Jocelyn Bell Burnell in 1967

pulsar is a rapidly rotating **neutron star**. The strong pulse comes as the rotating beam passes the Earth.

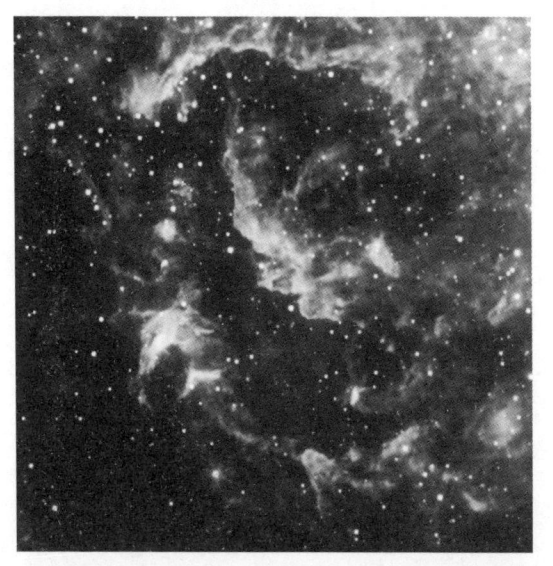

A pulsar: the spinning neutron star PSR B1509-58. It is about 17,000 light-years from Earth

By the way, in 2018 Jocelyn Bell Burnell was awarded a special prize in Physics, worth three million US dollars, for her discovery of radio pulsars. She donated all of the money to fund women, under-represented **ethnic minority** and **refugee** students to become physics researchers.

In 1977 a volunteer named Jerry Ehman was working at The Ohio

State SETI program, listening to radio signals from space. (Actually the signals were printed out and then the printouts were looked at – it's easier that way.)

Anyway, on this particular day Jerry Ehman saw a very **strong signal** received by the telescope. He drew a circle around the signal on the printout and wrote 'Wow!' next to it. People now call it the 'Wow!' signal.

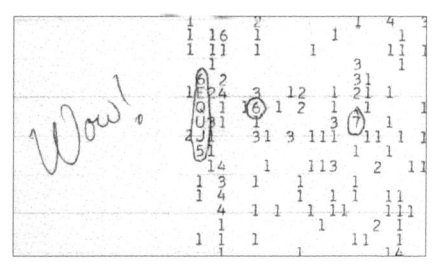

We still don't know what caused this signal, and it might indeed have been from aliens. The problem is that, after years of looking since then, we have never been able to 'hear' the same signal again. And one of the things that scientists think would show that a signal is from intelligent aliens is that it gets repeated.

The 'Wow!' signal

What if we didn't find any messages from aliens, but instead we found actual alien life? How would that be?

Well, in 1984 scientists in **Antarctica** found a **meteorite** that had come from the planet

The meteorite ALH8400

Mars. Named ALH8400, nobody paid much attention to it until 1996, when scientists looked at it under a powerful microscope. What they saw amazed them; it looked as though there were fossils of tiny **life forms** in the rock.

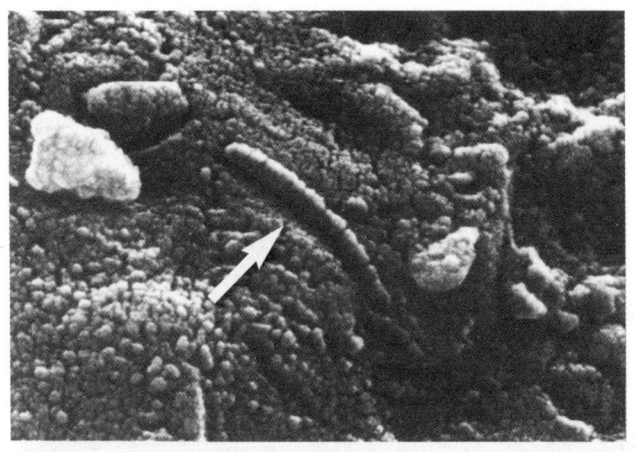

Are these fossils of alien life forms?

If this were true, it would be proof that, at one time in the past at least, there was life on Mars. (Scientists think the meteorite left Mars about 17 million years ago.)

But ... scientists are still arguing about this one even now. Some scientists say that there's not enough proof that it is (or was) life, and others say that they're convinced it is.

So we'll just have to wait and see. But, even if it does prove to be life, remember that the meteorite is very old and these are fossils, so it's no evidence that there is still life on Mars. And anyway, it's very primitive life – certainly not the intelligent life we'd like to meet.

On 4th October 1957 the first space-ship was sent from Earth into space. It was called **Sputnik 1**, a small unmanned **satellite** launched by Russia. For us humans, it was the beginning of the space age.

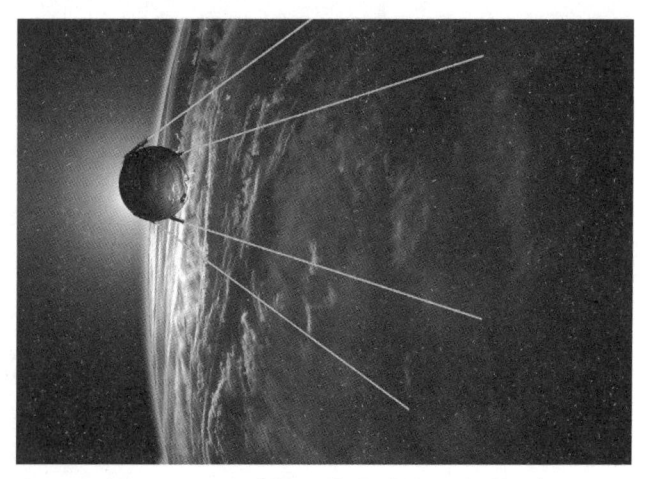

An artist's impression of Sputnik 1 orbiting the Earth

Since then there have been countless space flights, with unmanned probes and manned missions to launch satellites to make our televisions and mobile phones work, to explore our solar system, and even to put people on the Moon.

From our point of view – looking for aliens, one space mission stands out: the **Voyager** mission. In 1977 two robotic probes, **Voyager 1** and **Voyager 2**, were launched with the aim of

Voyager 2 (artist's impression)

exploring the distant planets in our solar system. Voyager 2 eventually visited the planets **Jupiter**, **Saturn**, **Uranus** and **Neptune** and taught us a huge amount about these planets.

Voyager 1 took a slightly different route, visiting Jupiter, Saturn and Saturn's largest moon, **Titan**.

As of 2019 both space probes have left our solar system and are now travelling in **interstellar space** at a speed of about 17 km per second. They have gone further than any other space craft ever launched from Earth.

Voyager 1 is the most distant of the two probes: it is now about 12 billion miles from Earth and it won't get close to another star system for about 40,000 years.

Voyager's Golden Records

The reason why the Voyager mission is of interest to us is because both space probes carried a 'Golden Record' – a long-playing (LP) disc. (This was the technology of the day – before CDs, long before mp3 files and long before streaming over the internet.)

NASA's Golden Record. The cover (left) includes instructions on how to play the disc, plus additional information

Each golden record was accompanied by a disc player (to play it on) and a set of instructions. The idea was that if the space probes met any aliens on their travels, the aliens could read the instructions, play the record and hear the sounds of planet Earth.

Each disc contained 117 pictures, humpback whale sounds, greetings from Earth in 54 different languages, a 20-minute 'sound essay' about life on Earth, and a 90-minute sampler of different kinds of music from planet Earth.

But what would an alien civilisation make of all this? Would they be able to read and understand the instructions? Even if they

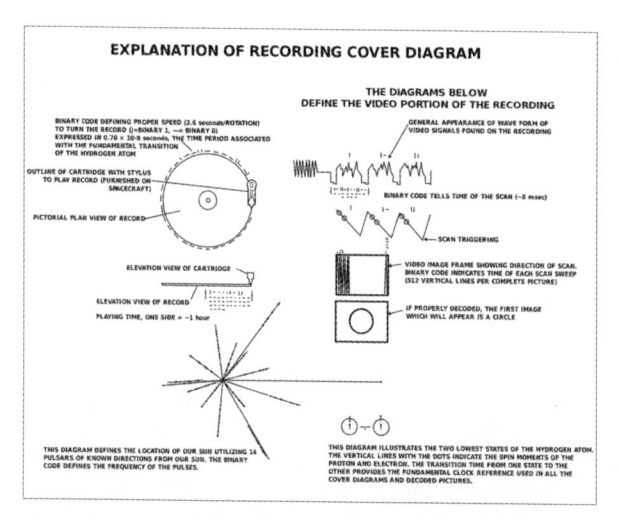

An explanation of the information contained on the cover of the golden record

could, greetings in 54 different languages might just sound to them like a lot of arguing, or like creatures in distress. If the aliens even have ears, of course.

To be honest, Voyager's golden records were designed, I think, more to say something to all humans on Earth than to alien ears. When these probes were launched, scientists were beginning to realise that the universe was a big place and would no doubt be full of wonders – including, possibly, alien life. The golden records were a way of saying to humans everywhere, 'Hey, this is exciting! Have you thought about what might be out there? Stop squabbling amongst yourselves and think about what it would mean to meet life elsewhere in the universe.'

Messages that wait

If sending messages to a planet or star system is easier than actually travelling there, it is still not ideal. The problem is that messages need somebody to be listening for them at the time that they are sent (or rather, at the time that they are received). Of course, you can keep sending the message over and over again, on repeat, but can you keep doing that for say millions of years?

What about sending a message that sits and waits to be discovered? In the 1968 film **2001: A Space Odyssey**, humans have built a base on the Moon. They discover a huge black rectangular object buried on the Moon; it's obviously not natural and must have been made by intelligent life. When the humans approach it, it sends a very powerful signal out towards Jupiter. The message to the humans is clear: 'Follow this signal.'

The film doesn't tell us, but it's pretty clear that the object was placed on the Moon by an advanced alien species with the technology to do this.

I think we can assume that the aliens in the film must have visited Earth at some point in the past and seen early, primitive life. They 'planted' the black object on the Moon, to wait until a species on Earth had evolved/developed enough to find it. (You need to be an intelligent species to be able to travel into space.)

This is a good solution to the 'message' problem. Can you imagine the universe being full of little hidden messages like this, all waiting to be discovered?

The Drake equation

Frank Drake, born in 1930, is an America astronomer who has been involved in the search for extraterrestrial intelligence for a large part of his life. He is one of the most important people involved in **SETI**.

In 1961 he wrote a mathematical **equation**, as a way to work out the

Professor Frank Drake

number of alien civilisations in our galaxy, **The Milky Way**. This quickly became famous and is now known as The Drake equation.

Why did he do it? Well, he didn't do it to work out the exact number of alien civilisations in The Milky Way. I know, he knew and by now I hope that you also know, that we don't have nearly enough information about aliens or about The Milky Way to be able to do that.

The Milky Way. How many alien civilisations?

No, he wrote The Drake equation for two other reasons. First, he wanted to get just a rough idea of what the answer might be. *Roughly* how many alien civilisations might there be in The Milky Way? Is it **one**? (That would be us, then.) Is it **one thousand**? **One million**? **One trillion**? More?

Second, he wanted to use the equation as a way to start a discussion amongst scientists, getting them to think about this question and how to get a better answer.

So what is the Drake equation? Well, I've written it on the opposite page, first in words, then at the bottom in the form he wrote it (which you definitely don't need to worry about!).

$$N = R_* \times f_p \times n_e \times f_l \times f_i \times f_c \times$$

The Drake equation

The number of alien civilisations in our galaxy that we might be able to communicate with is:

The average rate at which new stars are being formed in our galaxy, **times**

The fraction of those stars that have planets, **times**

The average number of planets that could support life, for each star that has planets, **times**

The fraction of planets that could support life that actually do develop life at some point, **times**

The fraction of planets with life that actually go on to develop intelligent life (civilisations), **times**

The fraction of civilisations that develop a technology that releases detectable signs of their existence into space, **times**

The length of time for which such civilizations release detectable signals into space.

For the maths nerds amongst you, the equation is:

$$N = R_* \times f_p \times n_e \times f_l \times f_i \times f_c \times L$$

It all looks a bit horrible, but actually it's pretty simple and covers most of the things we've been discussing in this book.

What Frank Drake is saying is that the number of **alien civilisations** in the Milky Way depends on, first of all, the number of **stars** in the Milky Way (plus the number of new stars being formed). Then, for those stars, we need to look at how many of them have **planets**. Because not all of them will.

How many planets will develop intelligent life?

Then, for those planets, how many of them could support **life**? Now, just because a planet *could* support life, that doesn't mean that life will automatically start there. So, for the planets that *could* support life, how many of them do actually go on to develop life at some point?

Then, for the planets that do manage to develop life, how many of them develop **intelligent life**?

Then, for the planets that do develop intelligent life, how

many of these intelligent civilisations manage to send signals or **messages** out into space?

And finally, we need to think about the length of time that these civilisations are around and sending messages into space. They need to be sending them when we're here listening! Sending a message ten million years ago isn't a lot of use to us, because we weren't here then to receive it.

Multiply all that together and you get your answer!

The trouble is that, although these are good questions to ask, and it's a good equation, we don't have enough information to fill in the numbers and get a useful answer.

Some scientists have tried to work out an answer to the equation, but they've had to make lots of **assumptions**. Their answers have ranged from 20 civilisations in the Milky Way to about fifty million!

How could we say 'Hello'?

Let's say we were going to send a message to an alien civilisation. Let's say we could either send a **radio message** into space, or we could put a message in a **space probe** and fire it off into space, in the hope that an intelligent alien civilisation finds it.

What message would we send?

Well, there's not a lot of point in sending a message that says something like, 'Hello, we come in peace,' or, 'Take us to your leader,' or anything like that. They probably wouldn't speak English and they might not understand what we mean by 'peace' or 'leader'.

Aliens and Earthlings welcome

Surely it would be better to keep it simple. It would be best to send a message that says, 'Here's a message that could only come from intelligent life. It's not random space noise. It's intelligent life trying to communicate with you.' We could also tell them where we are in the universe. (How would we do that?)

So what message would we send? It's actually quite a tricky problem. We couldn't send a message in any human **language** (English or Chinese, and so on) because we can be sure that they wouldn't understand it. We need to send a message using some kind of **universal language**.

What about the language of **mathematics**? That's universal. We're pretty sure, for example, that three times nine equals 27 whether you're on Earth, on the Moon or anywhere else in the universe. That's definitely universal.

We could use **prime numbers**, for example. A prime number is one that can be divided only by itself or by one.

So three is a prime number (only 3 and 1 can multiply to make three: 3 x 1 = 3) but four isn't a prime number (because 1 x 4 = 4, but 2 x 2 = 4 as well. So four can be divided by 1, 2 and 4.)

Prime numbers are very interesting, and we can be sure that alien civilisations would be interested in them too.

What if we sent them a list of all the prime numbers, say, up to 100? This is the list:

**1   3   5   7   11   13   17   19   23   29   31
37   41   43   47   53   59   61   67   71   73   79
83   89   97**

I'm pretty sure our aliens would spot that these are all prime numbers.

Alternatively we could send them another very important mathematical number: the value of **pi**. Do you know what pi is? It is sometimes written like this:

$$\pi$$

What is pi? First, measure the **circumference** of a circle (that's all the way around the outside) and also measure the **diameter** (in the diagram it's the line cutting the circle in half). If you then divide the circumference measurement by the diameter, you will *always* get the same number as an answer. This number we call pi.

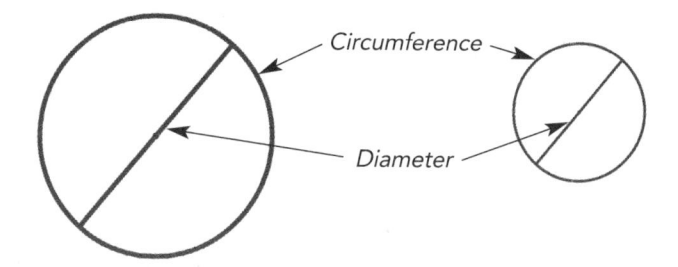

The number you get for pi is roughly 3.1416. It doesn't matter how big or how small the circle is – the answer is always pi.

This really seems to be a universal mathematical rule, so it would be good to show the aliens that we know the number pi. They would definitely know it too (unless they haven't discovered the circle – which is pretty unlikely).

Of course we couldn't tell them 'pi' or use the symbol π, because those are just names that we humans have given to this number. But we could tell them the number itself; they'd definitely recognise that.

Both of these suggestions (**prime numbers** and **pi**) show that there are definitely some universal maths numbers that we could send to our alien neighbours. They'd recognise these numbers immediately and would know that they had been sent by intelligent life.

The trouble is, both of these suggestions have a problem. The problem is to do with the **numbers** themselves.

And here's the problem: mathematics is universal, definitely, but the way we write down numbers isn't. To show you why, let's start by writing down the sequence of numbers from one to say eleven. We get this:

1   2   3   4   5   6   7   8   9   10   11

That seems straightforward. Well, up to a point it is. We have a different symbol for each number up to nine, then to get the next number (ten) we go back to use the same symbols again, putting a one to the left and a zero to the right, to get **10**.

Why do we do this? Because our counting system works to what we call **base-10**. In other words, when we get to 'ten' we start our sequence again with a one and a zero.

We could write out the same sequence of numbers (one to eleven) using (say) **base-6**. Then it would look like this:

1   2   3   4   5   10   11   12   13   14   15

(In base-6, we start our sequence again with a one and a zero once we have got to 'six'.)

Or we could use base-3:

1 2 10 11 12 20 21 22 30 31 32

(In base-3, we start our sequence again with a one and a zero once we have got to 'three'. So in base-3, for example, the number we call nine is written as 30.)

Or we could write the numbers in **base-2** (which is the counting system that computers use – it's called **binary**). Then our numbers one to eleven would look like this:

**1 10 11 100 101 110 111
1000 1001 1010 1011**

(In base-2, we start our sequence again with a one and a zero once we have got to 'two'. So in base-2, for example, the number nine is written as 1001.)

You can see immediately that a number written **12**, for example, means what we call 'twelve' in base-10, but in base-6 it means what we call 'eight' and in base-3 it means what we call 'five'. In base-2 it doesn't even exist.

So it's not going to be possible for us to write down any numbers, such as a list of prime numbers or the value of π, and expect our aliens to know what they mean, unless we know what base our aliens are themselves using.

Why do we use base-10 for our number system? It's simple really – it's because we have ten **fingers** and **thumbs** on our two hands, and before calculators it meant that we could use our hands to help us count accurately.

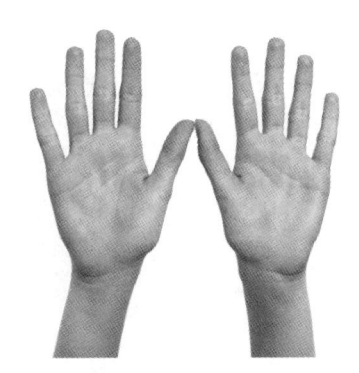

Why we use base-10

Not all human civilisations use base-10, though. The ancient **Maya** civilisation in South America, for example, used a base-20 system. (This might have been because they used all 20 of their fingers and toes.)

The Maya civilisation. Left: The Temple of Kukulcan at Chichen Itza, Mexico. Right: the Maya word for 'jaguar'

It is also said that the **Yuki** people in California and the **Pame** people in Mexico both use a base-8 counting system, because they count using the spaces between their fingers, rather than their fingers themselves.

This problem with numbers and the counting system that our aliens might use isn't impossible to solve. We could, for example,

If our aliens looked like this, for example, then they might be using a base-3 or a base-6 number system.

send our message in **binary**, as a series of ones and zeros. With only two symbols in the message (**1** and **0**), they might guess that we are sending a binary, or base-2 message.

But the problem does show how difficult it is to find a message that we can be sure will mean something to the civilisation that is receiving it.

Do we really want to meet aliens?

Have you thought about what it would mean for all of us on Earth if we did actually make contact with an advanced alien civilisation?

If it happened, it would mean that we would know for certain that we are not alone in the universe. Some people say that finding out we are not alone in the universe would be a very good thing for the human race. They say that it might help in stopping all the wars and petty fighting here on Earth, and would force governments to work together.

But could meeting advanced aliens be a bad thing?

The physicist **Stephen Hawking** definitely thought so. He said that any extraterrestrial civilisation we meet is likely to be much more advanced than we are.

Stephen Hawking

He pointed out that in the history of our own planet, every time a more advanced civilisation met a less advanced one, the less advanced people suffered very badly indeed. In fact, in most cases, their civilisation was wiped out.

The example that most people use is when **European** explorers 'discovered' the **New World** (as they called it – we call it **America**) in the fifteenth century. The most famous of these explorers was **Christopher Columbus**.

Christopher Columbus

The explorers brought new

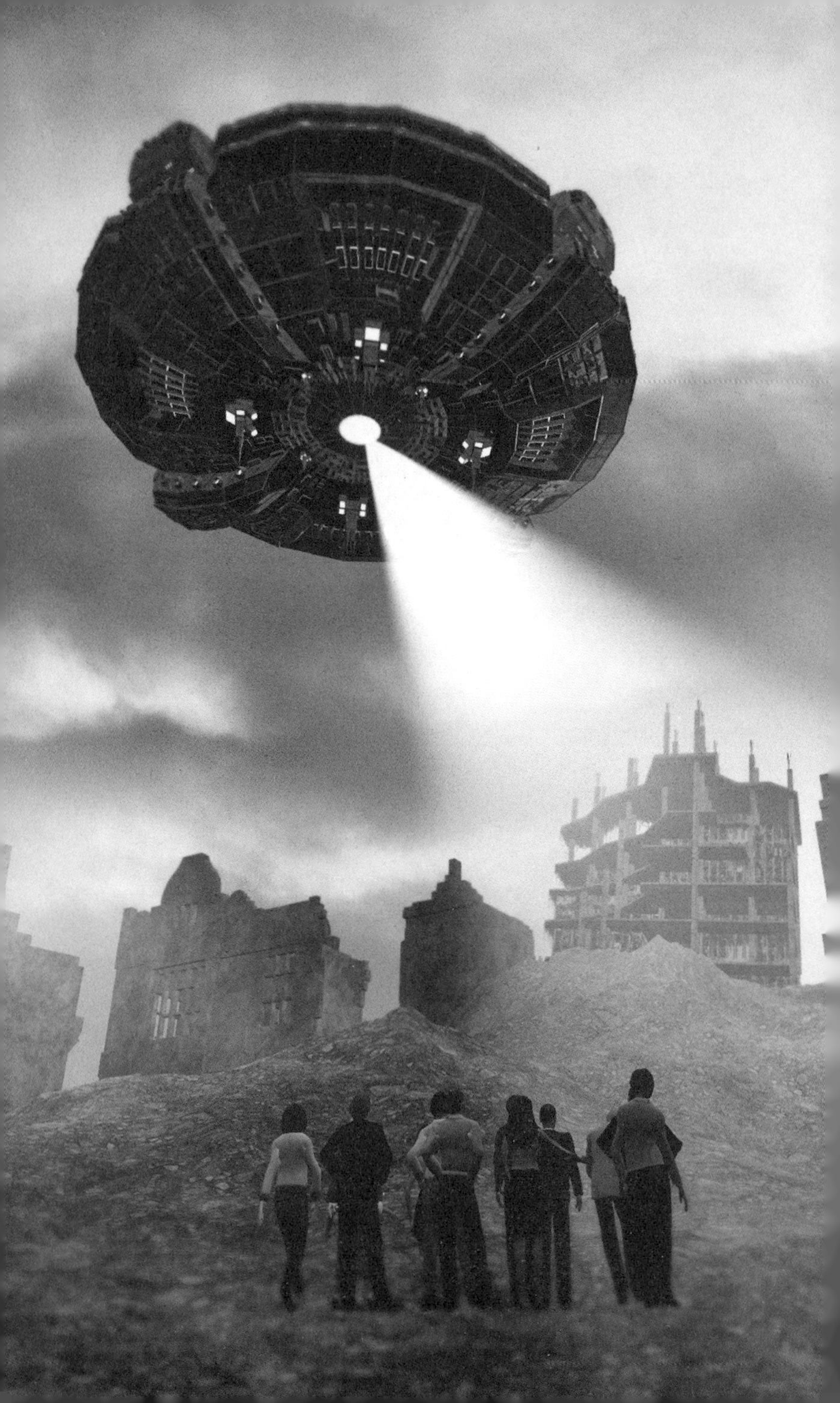

diseases to the New World, which the local people had no defence against. Historians think that between 80 and 95 per cent of the local population were killed by disease in this way.

The Europeans also brought their systems of running the country and owning land, and they made **slaves** of the local people. They also regarded everything in the New World as belonging to them, so they **pillaged** the land for **silver**, **gold** and other things of value.

Is it possible that alien visitors to planet Earth might treat us in the same way? They might just think of Earth as a place to come and get **resources** that they need, such as **oil**, **gas**, **water** – and **slaves**.

Perhaps we should just keep quiet and hope that nobody out there notices us.

Left: is this how it might end?

" We may never get there. But it will be fun trying. "

Ian Stewart

HAVE WE GOT IT ALL WRONG?

I think we've pretty much wrapped up our aliens conversation. Hopefully you'll agree that we've arrived at some useful conclusions and some even more useful **perspectives** on the chances of our actually meeting aliens.

Of course there's still a lot we don't know, but now we have a better idea of the things that we don't know, and of the things that we'll need to get answers to, before we can say anything more useful about the chances of our meeting aliens.

But what if we've got it all wrong?

A lot of books like this have a **Further reading** section at the back, with suggestions for other books to read as a follow-up.

Rather than doing that, I thought it might be more interesting to include a **Further thinking** section instead, with some **provocative** ideas, questions and thoughts. These are things to think about once you've finished the book.

So although this chapter is called , 'Have we got it all wrong?', think of it as also having a subtitle, too: 'Further thinking'.

What follows are a number of **disconnected** questions, thoughts and suggestions. Each one is perhaps the beginning of a different conversation (or even a different book) and a lot of these questions have **no solution** (or at least, not yet). If you've read all of this book, you'll be in a good position to tackle what follows.

So here we go.

Carbon versus silicon

All life on planet Earth is based on the element **carbon**. Carbon is an essential component of all life on Earth and, in addition, it is very common throughout the universe.

For a long time scientists assumed that all life in the universe would be based on carbon, but more recently scientists have realised that the element **silicon** (which in many ways is very similar to carbon) could also form the basis for life.

So is it possible that silicon-based **life forms** might have evolved elsewhere in the universe, in the same way that carbon-based life evolved on Earth?

There is another way that silicon-based life could emerge as well, although at the moment this is more the stuff of

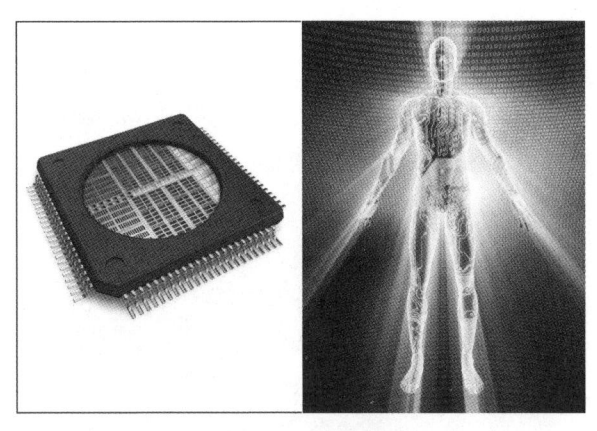

Left: computer chips are made of silicon.
Right: will we ever see silicon-based life forms?

science-fiction stories than real science. The **computer chips** in our computers, mobile phones, televisions, cars and everything else are all made out of silicon.

Is it possible that we will soon be designing and building computers that are so powerful that we will be able to call them **intelligent**?

Is it possible that these computers would be able to improve their own designs, themselves building better and more powerful computers, without humans getting involved at all?

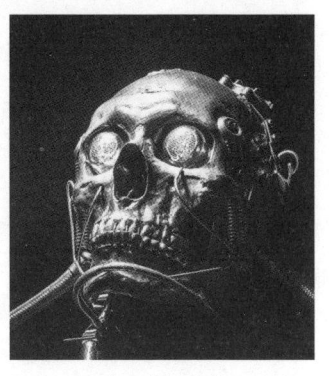

Designed and built by computers?

If they ever reached that stage, would they effectively be **replicating** themselves?

Would that be the beginning of computer **evolution**, real **artifical intelligence** (**AI**) and silicon-based life, here on Earth?

No reason to be afraid?

If it was the beginning of silicon-based life on Earth, should carbon-based life have any reason to be afraid?

No bodies

We have assumed that alien life will have **bodies** and brains, just like us. Is it possible that that's not the case?

As a very advanced type of alien life form became more and more intelligent, is it possible that it might lose the need to have a body at all? Is it possible that life, living things, could exist without bodies to live in?

An advanced alien species could be as different from humans as we are from mushrooms growing in the forest.

They could be as different from us as we are from mushrooms

Here's an alternative way of asking the same question: if humans continue to **evolve** (and if we manage to avoid destroying ourselves completely), what will we look like in say a hundred million years from now?

Life without mercy

Is it possible that there could be an advanced form of alien life that we cannot communicate with and that is not interested in communicating with us?

It could be a very **efficient** form of life that doesn't need to communicate and doesn't need to debate or discuss. It just *does*. It could still have highly advanced technology, but in most other ways it wouldn't be anything like our definitions of advanced life. It could behave like an **apex predator**, a creature at the top of its **food chain** that fears nothing and shows no emotions, acting without mercy.

This would be an extremely dangerous species to come into contact with.

Unexpected messages

Some scientists have said that they are surprised that, after many decades of looking and listening, we have not yet encountered any alien civilisations. But is it possible that we are looking in the wrong places for the wrong things?

Is it possible that there are 'messages' that aliens could be sending out that we have not thought about? 'Messages' that it didn't occur to us might be messages?

In 1995 scientists discovered that the star **KIC 8462852**, also known as **Tabby's Star**, (it's approximately 1,500 light-years from Earth) was getting dimmer as time passed. This isn't particularly unusual, but what *was* unusual was the fact that the star was getting dimmer by about 15 - 20%, which is a huge amount.

For a star to get 20% dimmer, something about half the size of the star would need to be blocking it, stopping the light reaching us. There was nothing we knew of in science that could explain that.

Was it possible that an alien civilisation was constructing a huge **megastructure** in space, in front of the star, to make the light dim so massively?

Why would they do this? Well, they might do it for reasons of their own (such as building a giant city in space, or building some kind of structure to capture **energy**, for example).

Or they might do it in order to send a message to other intelligent life in the universe. After all, any other intelligent civilisation that noticed a 20% dip in the brightness of a star would immediately realise that this couldn't be a natural thing.

And the benefit of course is that these other alien civilisations would know exactly where the aliens sending the message were located – well, at least to the nearest star!

An artist's impression of the star KIC8462852, showing the solution to the puzzle: a massive dust cloud

Was this dimming star a message from aliens – a kind of message that we hadn't thought about before?

In this case, sadly not. Scientists have now established that the light from the star was being blocked by a massive dust cloud.

But this was a bit of a wake-up call for **SETI**-watchers. When a message arrives, it might not be in the form we'd been expecting!

Technology blinkers

When we think about the kinds of **technology** that an advanced alien civilisation might have, it seems that quite often what we expect them to have is just a better version of what we have.

In the 1950s, for example, there was a lot of public interest in the idea of building space-ships to explore space. (The first space probe, **Sputnik 1**, left Earth in 1957.) Science fiction stories of the time therefore tended to focus on aliens arriving in very advanced space-ships.

As our technology developed over the decades, aliens were always described in terms of human technology: their technology was just like ours, but it was better. They had weapons just like ours, but their weapons were more powerful; the armour on their space-ships was just like ours, but again, it was better. Not different, but better.

But alien technology is likely to be very different indeed. It will almost certainly be better than ours, too – a lot better – but it will be different.

Take one example that always surprises me: when aliens invade Earth in fiction films/TV programmes, they always seem to go from city to city, blowing up all the buildings and shooting all the people using big, impressive weapons.

Really? Really?

How does shooting people get anything done? Unless of course the aliens want to kill every human being on Earth. In which case, since there are about seven billion people on our planet, shooting them all one by one is an awful lot of effort that is going to take a long, long time.

Isn't it more likely that aliens would have a simple, **global** solution that would either disable or kill all life on Earth? Perhaps something that they could put in the air or the water to get the job done. Or something much more **sophisticated** than that. It would be much less effort, and they wouldn't have to spend all that time blowing stuff up, either.

We need to think about where *their* technology is, not where ours is.

Progress

Sitting underneath most of the discussions in this book is the idea of **progress**. We like to assume that progress is behind nearly everything around us. Planets form, life starts, life becomes more complex, intelligent life emerges, technology gets developed. It's all progress.

But actually there is nothing that says that progress is **inevitable**. Nobody has been given any guarantees that the future is going to be better than the past.

For example, around 70 million years ago **dinosaurs** were the **dominant** species on Earth, and it seemed likely that this would continue for a long, long time.

But when a huge asteroid (about 10 - 15 km across) crashed into the Earth around 66 million years ago, it changed everything. Clouds of dust blocked out the Sun for years, and it is estimated that about 75% of all **species** on Earth went **extinct** as a result. The dinosaurs were virtually wiped out.

Here's another example. We know that at some point in the past the planet **Mars** had plenty of liquid water on its surface, and it also had an **atmosphere**. It may also have had the beginnings of primitive life.

Yet now Mars has lost nearly all of its atmosphere and there is little or no liquid water on the surface. At one time it might have looked as if life was going to thrive there, but now Mars looks like a dead planet.

A dead planet? The surface of Mars. Photo taken in 2016 by the Mars Curiosity rover

Our science is wrong

I think it's fair to say that we don't *think* our science is wrong; we *know* it's wrong. The problem is that we don't know which bits are wrong, and we don't know how to make them 'right'.

For as long as people have been looking at the world around them, they have been trying to explain why the world is the way it is. When **Isaac Newton** published his **laws of gravity** in 1687, and they were found to make accurate **predictions**, everybody regarded it as a great scientific achievement (which it was).

Isaac Newton is supposed to have thought of the laws of gravity when he saw an apple fall from a tree. The story probably isn't true

But were Newton's laws 'correct'? Were they the laws that the universe followed? Did the planets 'use' Newton's laws to work out where they should be in space? No, of course not.

Newton's laws were very good at explaining why things moved as they did, and they allowed us to **predict** how planets and even objects on Earth would move, but they were only an **explanation**.

In fact, over time we realised that Newton's laws of gravity worked most of the time, but not quite all of the time. (For example, Newton's laws could not accurately explain the motions of the planet **Mercury** around the **Sun** – see page 67.)

When **Einstein** came along with his explanation of gravity at the beginning of the 20th Century, he threw out Newton's ideas of action at a distance and replaced them with theories about **space-time**, **relativity** and rubber sheets. Einstein's revolutionary theories were also able to explain correctly the orbit of Mercury.

Albert Einstein in 1947

So did the universe suddenly stop following Newton's theories and follow Einstein's instead? Of course not. The universe carried on as normal.

So can we be sure that Einstein's theories are right and Newton's are wrong? Again no, of course not. Einstein's theories are closer to what we **observe** in the real world than Newton's, but that doesn't make them right. The theories we have now are no more than the best **explanations** we have for why things work the way the do; nobody can give us any guarantees that these theories are right.

So what scientists are doing now is just what scientists have always done: they are focusing in on the areas where there is a difference between what their theories predict and what they see in the real world. Because those are the areas where our science has got to be wrong – or, more likely, **incomplete**. (Usually our theories can explain *part* of what is happening, but not all of it.)

Let's look at a few examples.

Dark matter

When scientists look at the way that rotating **galaxies** behave, they find that these galaxies aren't obeying the **laws of gravity**. According to our understanding of gravity, there isn't enough stuff (enough matter) in the galaxies to stop them flying apart as they rotate.

There are two solutions to this: either the laws of gravity aren't what we think they are, or there is more **stuff** inside each galaxy than we can see. (More stuff – that is, more matter – would give the galaxy a stronger gravitational pull, which would hold the galaxy together and stop everything flying off into space.)

Most scientists have ruled out the first possibility, because the laws of gravity that we use seem to be making very good predictions about the rest of the universe. So we think they are pretty reliable. That leaves the second possibility: there is more stuff inside these galaxies than we can see.

So what is this stuff? Well, scientists have no idea: they can't see it and they can't detect it. But they think it exists. So they've called it **dark matter**, which is a pretty good name for it.

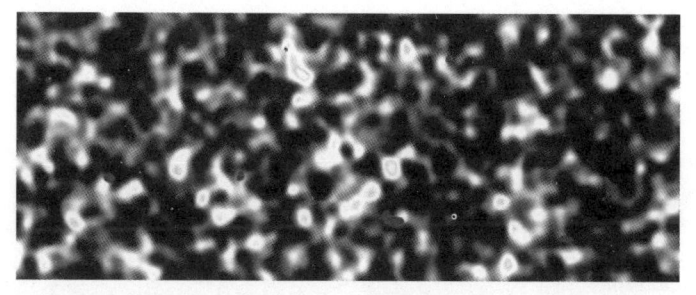

A map of part of the sky showing where scientists think dark matter might be. Dark matter is shown as the lighter (but not white) patches

How much dark matter is there? Well, if our understanding of gravity is correct, then dark matter would make up about 85% of all of the matter in each galaxy. That's a lot of extra matter!

There are lots of theories about what could make up this dark matter, but so far we haven't been able to prove any of these theories right.

Dark energy

In Chapter Four we discussed how **Edwin Hubble** discovered that the universe is expanding. This was the start of a revolution in our understanding of the universe, which led to our theories about the **Big Bang**.

Well, since the 1990s scientists have realised that the speed at which the universe is **expanding** is actually increasing. In other words, the universe is getting bigger at a faster rate now that it was in the past. The speed at which things are moving away from each other is increasing.

The universe is expanding faster than it should be. (Just to be clear: this is not a picture of the universe)

The problem is that scientists think that this should not be happening. Again, the explanation seems to be that either our laws of gravity are wrong, or there is some kind of force that we don't know about that is helping to push all the stuff in the universe apart, making the universe expand faster than we think it should.

Again scientists have gone for the second option: they think there is a force that they don't know about that is pushing stuff apart. They have called this force **dark energy**. And, just as with dark matter, scientists don't know what it is and so far haven't been able to detect it.

It is interesting that scientists used to think that the universe would expand following the **Big Bang**, but eventually the force of **gravity** would pull everything back together again, so the universe would slow its rate of expansion and then start to **contract**; the universe would start to get smaller. Finding out that the universe is actually expanding faster than they expected has changed their thinking about the future of the universe.

Quantum mechanics

Scientists have two sets of theories at the moment that explain how the world works. Einstein's **theory of relativity** has very good explanations for gravity and the motions of planets, galaxies and the expanding universe. In other words, it explains all the big stuff pretty well. (OK, there are a few funnies, such as dark matter and dark energy.)

Then there is a separate theory called **quantum mechanics** (which we haven't talked about in this book). That theory explains how very small things such as **atoms** behave.

The problem is that these two theories have very different explanations of how the world we live in works, and they can't both be right.

What's worse, both theories *seem* to be right. For example, scientists use quantum mechanics to design things like **computer chips**. Surely if quantum mechanics were wrong, we couldn't use it to build computers. (We're not saying that computers don't exist, are we?)

The only obvious answer, the way of **reconciling** these two theories, is to say that they are both part of a different, bigger **explanation** of reality that we haven't discovered yet.

This man, Max Planck, is regarded as the father of quantum mechanics

Faster than light travel?

One experiment that's been done with quantum mechanics is particularly worrying. It involves firing two tiny particles (called **electrons**) off in opposite directions. These two particles are what scientists call **quantum entangled** (don't worry about it), which means that whatever you do to the one particle, happens to the other one as well.

The problem is that it happens to the second particle instantly – and I mean *instantly*. It doesn't matter how far apart the two particles are.

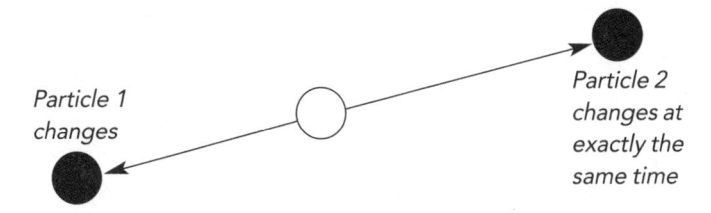

Particle 1 changes

Particle 2 changes at exactly the same time

We do not understand quantum entanglement

So we think that, even if the two particles are billions of light-years apart, if one particle is changed, the other particle immediately changes too. Somehow the information that the first particle has changed gets to the second particle instantly. The information is not even taking the speed of light to get there.

This seems to make no sense at all and we have no idea how it happens; we only know that it does happen (we've proved it in experiments).

Is it possible that finding the answer to this little problem might be the key to unlocking a whole new world of **faster than light** travel? Some scientists are very excited about this!

Revolutionary changes?

Is it possible that some of the basic things we take for granted in science might turn out to be wrong?

For example, we think about **time** as being something like a river that is constantly moving forward, never backward. But what if time doesn't work like that. What if some things could exist outside of time?

Does time flow like a river? Could some things exist outside of time?

Or what if, for example, we discovered that the force of **gravity** had been changing over time? What if, early in the universe, it was much stronger, or much weaker, than it is now?

Or what if we don't live in a world of three **dimensions**, but instead live in a world with ten, or eleven, or 30 dimensions?

Multiple universes

Some scientists have suggested that there isn't just one universe. Rather, they suggest, there are lots of universes, and together with our universe they make up everything that exists. They call all these universes together the **multiverse**.

We cannot even imagine what a multiverse would look like

The idea is that these other universes exist at the same time as ours, in parallel with it. (Scientists sometimes talk about **parallel universes**.)

Some scientists have even suggested that some of these parallel universes might have laws of physics that are different to those in our own universe.

It has even been suggested that some of these other

universes might have more than three **dimensions**; 10 or 11 dimensions are popular suggestions (not because it sounds good, but because the mathematics suggests that).

Of course the big problem is, how can we find out? Is there any way of seeing, or getting messages from, any of these other universes? At the moment nobody has any idea how to start looking.

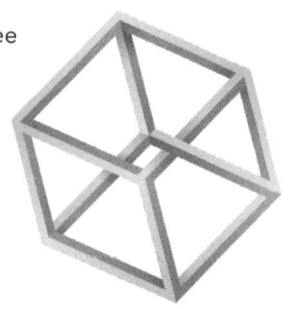

How do you imagine a world with more than three dimensions?

Is a theory you can't ever investigate still a scientific theory?

The Big Crunch

If the idea of multiple universes isn't mind-boggling enough, then how about this.

Nearly all scientists agree that our universe started with the **Big Bang**, in the way I've described in Chapter Four. One theory these scientists have is that the universe started with the Big Bang, with everything expanding out from the starting point. But then this expansion would gradually slow down, as the force of gravity began to pull all the stuff in the universe back together. Eventually the universe would start to **contract** as a result of this gravitational force.

After a long, long time, the universe would contract back to a single point again – something scientists call the **Big Crunch**.

Then everything (and when I say 'everything', I mean the entire universe) would start over again, with another Big Bang.

So the history of the universe might be a series of Big Bangs and Big Crunches, with the universe expanding and contracting in between each one, just as if it was breathing.

Recently, however, scientists have realised that the universe doesn't look as if it's going to contract at all – it seems to be expanding ever more quickly. (That's the **dark energy** problem I described above.)

And that discussion takes on to one of the biggest questions of all: how and when will the universe end?

But that, I feel sure, must be the start of another book.

> "Language was invented so that people could conceal their thoughts from each other."

Charles-Maurice de Talleyrand

GLOSSARY

absolute zero Minus 273.15 degrees Celsius. We think that this is the coldest temperature possible, as atoms stop moving at this temperature.

Albert Einstein A very important scientist, born in 1879 in Germany. His theory of relativity changed the way we understand how the world works and gave a new, more accurate, explanation of gravity.

algorithm A set of rules for solving a problem or getting to a result. The rules are applied in steps, one at a time.

alien A living creature, or life form, that did not begin on planet Earth, but instead began elsewhere in the universe.

Almagest The encyclopaedia of mathematics put together by Ptolemy (who lived sometime around 150 CE).

amino acids Molecules containing carbon that we think are the building blocks of life.

ancient Egyptians An ancient civilisation that existed in the place we now call Egypt. It lasted from about 3100 BCE until 30 BCE.

Andromeda Galaxy The nearest galaxy to us (apart from the Milky Way, which we are part of). It is about 2.5 million light-years from Earth.

apex predator A predator that is at the top of its food chain. No other organisms hunt it, so it has nothing to fear.

Aristotle A very important ancient Greek philosopher. Born 384 BCE, died 322 BCE.

artificial intelligence (AI) Intelligence that has been created in machines (computers). Some people say that one day, with AI, you won't know whether you are talking to a machine or a human being.

asteroid An object that is smaller than a planet and which, like a planet, orbits the Sun.

astrobiology A new science looking at the possibility of life elsewhere in the universe.

astronomical unit (AU) A measurement of distance. One AU is the distance between the Earth and the Sun – roughly 150 million km.

bacteria Very small, simple organisms with just one cell. Bacteria are almost everywhere on Earth; millions live inside your body and help keep you healthy.

Big Bang A theory about how the universe began (with a huge explosion of matter from 'nothing'). Now accepted as the best explanation we have.

Big Crunch The idea that the universe might stop expanding and start to contract, in a reverse of the Big Bang. If this were to happen, everything might end in a Big Crunch.

biosphere On a planet, all the living and non-living things interacting together. It includes all the animals and plants, the atmosphere, the soil and rocks and even the climate.

black smokers Structures built of minerals that are found near hydrothermal vents on the sea floor.

carbon A chemical element. It is very common in the universe. It is the basis of all life on Earth and might form the basis of all life in the universe.

Celsius A measure of temperature. Also known as centigrade. The freezing point of water is 0 degrees Celsius; the boiling point of water is 100 degrees Celsius.

clockwork universe The idea that we live in a universe that is completely predictable and measurable.

CGI Computer Generated Imagery (used, for example, in films).

Charles Darwin A very important scientist who suggested the theory of evolution in his 1859 book called 'On the Origin of Species'. Born in 1809, he died in 1882.

COBE The COsmic Background Explorer satellite. Between 1989 and 1993 it collected data on the cosmic background radiation, the leftover signal from the Big Bang.

consciousness Being awake and aware of your surroundings; being able to think.

Copernicus Born 1473 in Poland. He wrote a book putting the Sun, not the Earth, at the centre of the universe, with the Earth, planets and stars moving around it in perfect circles. The book was not published until after his death.

cosmic background radiation The leftover energy from the Big Bang at the beginning of the universe. It was first detected in 1964 by the scientists Arno Penzias and Robert Wilson.

cosmic void The name we give to the huge gaps in the universe between superclusters.

creation myth A story about how the world began. Different groups of people around the world often have their own creation myths.

dark energy The extra energy that scientists think must exist in the universe to be making the universe expand faster than it 'ought' to be.

dark matter The extra 'stuff' that scientists think must be inside galaxies to explain why galaxies don't fly apart as they rotate.

Drake equation A mathematical formula written by the astronomer Frank Drake in 1961, to calculate the chances of our meeting aliens.

Earth The third planet from the Sun and our home. The only place in the universe where we know for sure that life exists.

Edwin Hubble An American astronomer (born 1889, died 1953). He discovered that the universe is expanding, and that the galaxies furthest away from us are moving away from us at the highest speed. He put forward Hubble's law.

ellipse A shape like a flattened circle.

elliptical galaxy A type of galaxy, named after its shape.

electromagnetism A theory put forward by James Clerk Maxwell. It said that electricity, magnetism and light were all waves that moved at the speed of light.

element A substance that is made from only one kind of atom. Elements cannot be broken down into anything simpler.

Enceladus A moon of the planet Saturn. Scientists think there might be life on Enceladus.

environment The air, water and land where creatures live.

epicycles Circles moving inside other moving circles (a way of explaining motion that wasn't circular, using circles).

Europa A moon of the planet Jupiter. Scientists think there might be life on Europa.

evolution A theory that explains how different species of plants and animals change or die out over long, long periods of time. The theory was first put forward by Charles Darwin. It is now accepted by nearly all scientists.

evolutionary advantage A change in an organism or species as a result of evolution that makes it better suited to its surroundings, so that it has an advantage in those surroundings.

excretion One of the seven criteria for life: living things can get rid of waste products that they don't need. (Humans do it when they go to the toilet.)

exomoon A moon orbiting a planet in another solar system.

exoplanet A large object that orbits a star in another solar system (that is, not in our solar system).

extinct When a particular species of animal has completely died out, so there are no more alive on Earth.

extraterrestrial Outside of, or beyond, our planet Earth. Not from our world.

fossil record All the different types of fossils that have been discovered, together with the information about them, such as where they were found and how old they are.

Frank Drake An American astronomer, born in 1930, who is an important figure in the search for extraterrestrial intelligence. He put forward the Drake equation.

(Sir) Fred Hoyle A British scientist who in 1948 suggested the Steady State theory of the origins of the universe. He also gave the Big Bang theory its name.

Gaia theory A theory suggested by the British scientist James Lovelock. The theory suggests that the living and non-living things on Earth work together as if they were a single system – almost like a single organism. The theory is not accepted by all scientists.

galactic year The time it takes a rotating galaxy to make one complete revolution.

galaxy Stars, solar systems, gas and dust tend to clump together in galaxies.

galaxy cluster A group of galaxies, all held together by gravity.

Galileo Galilei Born 1564 in Italy. He observed moons orbiting Jupiter, proving that not everything orbited the Earth. He was tried by the Catholic church for his views and forced to admit he was wrong (which he wasn't).

gene Information that is carried in an organism's cells that is passed on when that organism has babies. Genes are how children look like their parents, for example.

geological time A way of dividing the history of the Earth into different sections. Because the Earth is over 4 billion years old, geological time covers a very long period.

Goldilocks zone See habitable zone.

gravity A force that makes all things with mass tend to move towards each other. The laws of gravity were first put forward by Isaac Newton in 1687.

growth One of the seven criteria for life: living things can grow, making new living material for themselves.

habitable zone The part of a solar system where liquid water could exist. Too far away from the star and it is too cold for water; too close and the water boils away. The habitable zone is where life might be found. Sometimes called the Goldilocks zone.

Heinrich Olbers A German astronomer who pointed out that if the universe were infinite, the night sky should be as bright as daytime. This is called Olbers' paradox.

heresy Believing or suggesting a theory that goes against the accepted beliefs of a religious group or organisation.

hominid A group of creatures that we call the great apes. Hominids include humans, gorillas and chimpanzees – plus other related creatures that are now extinct.

Homo sapiens The scientific name for human beings.

Hubble telescope A space telescope launched in 1990. Named after Edwin Hubble.

Hubble's law The mathematical formula (discovered by Edwin Hubble) that links how far away from us a galaxy is and how quickly it is moving away from us. (Further away = faster.)

hydrothermal vents Fissures, or cracks, in the sea floor, from which very hot water continually shoots out. The water has been heated by the interior of our planet.

infinitesimal Very small; so small that it is impossible to measure it.

infinite The idea of something having no end or no limit; going on forever. Something that is infinite cannot be measured.

(Sir) Isaac Newton Born in 1642. A very important British scientist, working in many different areas. He put forward his laws of motion, he explained gravity and created the modern scientific method.

interstellar space The parts of the universe between different star systems, but still within the same galaxy.

James Clerk Maxwell A Scottish scientist, born 1831. Famous for his theory of electromagnetism.

James Lovelock A British scientist, born in 1919. He suggested the Gaia theory.

Jocelyn Bell Burnell An English scientist who in 1967 discovered a strong radio pulse coming from space. She had discovered a pulsar – but thought briefly that it might have been a message from aliens.

Jupiter Fifth planet from the Sun and largest planet in our solar system.

Kepler Johannes Kepler, born 1571 in Germany. He discovered that the orbits of planets are elliptical in shape, not circular.

Kepler 11 A distant star, 2,150 light-years from Earth. We believe it has six exoplanets orbiting it.

Laniakea supercluster The name we give to the supercluster that we are part of.

light-year A measurement of distance (not of time). It is the distance that light travels in one year: about 9.46 trillion km.

Local Group The name we give to the galaxy cluster that we are part of.

locomotion One of the seven criteria for life: living things can move.

Mars Fourth planet from the Sun. Often called the Red Planet because of its reddish colour.

medieval Relating to the historical period we call the Middle Ages – very roughly 450 to 1500 CE.

Mercury Closest planet to the Sun and the smallest planet in our solar system.

microfossils Fossils of tiny microorganisms. Microfossils that are 3.45 billion years old have been found on Earth.

microorganisms Microscopic organisms.

Miller – Urey experiment An experiment carried out by Stanley Miller and Harold Urey in 1953 to recreate what Earth was like when it was very young. They created a 'soup' of amino acids – the building blocks of life.

Milky Way The name for the galaxy that we are part of.

moon A large object that orbits a planet.

Moon Earth has one moon. We call it (confusingly) 'the Moon'.

multicellular organisms Organisms that have bodies that are made up of more than just one cell.

multiverse Some scientists have suggested that our universe is just one of many different universes, which together make up something they call the multiverse.

nanotechnology Building very small things by working with individual molecules and atoms.

NASA The US National Aeronautics and Space Administration, the organisation that carries out space exploration for the USA.

natural selection Animals that are best suited, or adapted, to the surroundings they live in will survive and have babies. Animals that are not so well adapted may not survive. This is natural selection. It is sometimes called 'survival of the fittest'. Natural selection is one of the three things necessary for evolution to take place.

Neptune The eighth planet in our solar system, and the planet furthest from the Sun.

neurons Also known as nerve cells. These are cells in the body that send messages to and from the brain. Neurons are part of an organism's nervous system.

neutron star A star that has collapsed to a very small size (about 30 km across).

Newtonian mechanics How scientists understand the way things move, based on Newton's laws of motion.

nutrition One of the seven criteria for life: living things can take in 'food' from outside their bodies.

observable universe That part of the universe that it is possible for us to see from Earth.

organic molecules Molecules that contain carbon. We think that organic molecules are the building blocks of life.

organism A living thing, or life form.

panspermia The theory that life exists almost everywhere in space. The theory suggests that life on Earth might have come from outer space.

Pharaoh Thutmose III A pharaoh (or king) of ancient Egypt, who ruled for 54 years from 1479 BCE to 1425 BCE.

pi (or π) The number you get when you divide the circumference of a circle by the diameter. The answer is always the same: about 3.1416. We call it pi (pronounced 'pie').

planet A large object that orbits a star. Planets that orbit stars in other solar systems are now called exoplanets.

Pluto A distant 'dwarf planet' orbiting the Sun. Until 2006 it was said to be the ninth planet from the Sun.

predator An animal that hunts for food.

prime number A number that can only be divided by itself and one. So 17 is a prime number (only 1 x 17=17) but 16 is not a prime number (4 x 4=16, 2 x 8=16 and 1 x 16=16).

primeval soup A 'soup' of amino acids – the building blocks of life – created in an experiment carried out by Harold Urey and Stanley Miller in 1953 to recreate what Earth was like when it was very young.

Principia Mathematica The Latin title of Newton's book 'Principles of Mathematics', published in 1687.

Proxima Centauri The nearest star to our solar system (not counting the Sun). It is 4.25 light-years away from Earth.

Proxima Centauri b An exoplanet discovered orbiting the star Proxima Centauri. Scientists think it is in the star system's habitable zone.

Ptolemy An astronomer and mathematician who lived around 150 BCE. He said that the Moon, the Sun and the planets all move around the Earth in perfect circles.

pulsar A rapidly rotating neutron star.

quantum mechanics A theory about how very small things such as atoms behave.

radio telescope A telescope that is rather like an ordinary telescope, except that it magnifies radio waves rather than light waves.

relativity Einstein's theory that describes gravity as a curvature of space-time (compared with Newton's explanation of gravity as a force acting at a distance).

replicator Something that can replicate, or make copies of itself. Humans are replicators, and so are some computer viruses.

reproduction One of the seven criteria for life: living things can make copies of themselves. Reproduction is also one of the three things necessary for evolution to take place.

respiration One of the seven criteria for life: living things can convert the food they take in into the energy they need.

Roswell, New Mexico A city in the USA where an alien space-ship is supposed to have crashed in 1947.

Saturn The sixth planet from the Sun and second-largest in our solar system. It is most famous for its rings.

senses One of the seven criteria for life: living things can sense the environment around them.

SETI Search for ExtraTerrestrial Intelligence. The name given to all scientific work on Earth searching for alien life.

singularity The single point (in space and in time) from which the universe started with the Big Bang, 13.8 billion years ago.

solar system A star, together with all the planets, moons and other objects that move around that star.

Solar System The name we give to the solar system that we are part of.

space-time In Einstein's theory of relativity, space and time are linked, in what he called space-time. Space-time is distorted, or curved, by heavy objects.

species The word biologists use to describe different kinds of living things.

spiral galaxy A type of galaxy, named after its shape.

Sputnik 1 The first space-ship sent from Earth into space (in October 1957). It was unmanned.

Steady State theory A theory about the origins of the universe. It said that the universe had always existed and always will exist, in a 'steady state'. Now shown to be incorrect.

supercluster A group of galaxy groups, or galaxy clusters, all held together by gravity.

survival of the fittest See natural selection.

Tabby's star A star 1,500 light-years from Earth. Scientists thought for a while that it might be the source of an alien message. It isn't.

tardigrade Also known as a water bear or moss piglet. Tiny creatures (about half a millimetre long) that seem to be able to survive in places that would kill other creatures.

technology Things that are produced as a result of scientific knowledge (e.g. pencils, space-ships, computers, kettles).

Tycho de Brahe An eccentric Danish nobleman who helped Johannes Kepler. De Brahe is best known because he had his nose sliced off in a duel.

unidentified flying object (UFO) A flying object in the sky (or in space) that we have not been able to identify.

universe The universe contains everything that exists. It includes all the stars, planets, galaxies, etc.

Uranus The seventh planet from the Sun.

variation When living things make copies of themselves, but the copies are a little bit different to the parent(s). Variation is one of the three things necessary for evolution to take place.

Venus Second planet from the Sun.

virus A very small 'thing' that can be found inside the cells of organisms. Some scientists think that viruses cannot be classified as 'living'; other scientists disagree.

Voyager The mission to explore the distant parts of our solar system. There were two space probes, Voyager 1 and Voyager 2. Both have now left our solar system.

wormhole A possible way of taking a shortcut through space and time. Wormholes might make time travel possible, but nobody knows if they really exist.

> "Science is a way of thinking, much more than it is a body of knowledge."

Carl Sagan

WORD LIST

absolute
achievements
advantage
ambitious
assumptions
billion
carbon dioxide
classified
conclusive
contract
curious
data
dense

accurate
advanced
adventurer
arrogant
atmosphere
camouflage
chaos
concentric
consequences
criteria
curvature
definition
design solution

detect	diameter
dictionary	dimensions
directional	disconnected
distort	dominant
effectively	elliptical
emitted	emotions
encyclopaedia	energy
entire	essential
ethnic minority	eventually
explanation	finite
fluctuations	friction
generation	global
heat signature	immobile
implications	inevitable
infer	influence
Inquisition	intention
invisible	judgment
lasers	literally
magnification	measurable
megastructure	microscopic
million	nuclear weapons
nuclear waste	observation
observe	offspring
opportunity	oxygen
parallel	patent
perspective	pillaged

population	predictable
predictions	presence
primitive	probabilities
process	profound
progress	proof
proposal	protective
provocative	pulpit
quintillion	radical
reconciling	refugee
relative distances	resources
rethink	ridiculous
rotate	round trip
science-fiction	septillion
social behaviour	solution
sophisticated	static
stationary	structure
suburbs	synchronised
technology	telescope
theoretically	thrived
timescale	tradition
trillion	typical
underlying	uninhabitable
unobservable	variations
vary	witchcraft

"Our scientific power has outrun our spiritual power. We have guided missiles and misguided men."

Martin Luther King, Jr.

IMAGE CREDITS

Chapter 1 Where are They?
Page 12: iStock.com/cosmin4000.

Chapter 2 Three Choices
Page 17: **iStock.com/CSA Images; Roswell Daily Record;** *page 18*: **Chipdawes;** *page 20*: **Bruno Comby** - licensed under the Creative Commons Attribution-Share Alike 1.0 Generic (https://creativecommons.org/licenses/by-sa /1.0/deed.en) license; *page 21*: **iStock.com/gecko753;** *page 23*: **Rogers AD, Tyler PA, Connelly DP, Copley JT, James R, et al.** - licensed under the Creative Commons Attribution 2.5 Generic (https:// creativecommons.org/ licenses/by/2.5/deed.en) license; *page 24*: **NOAA Okeanos Explorer Program, Galapagos Rift Expedition 2011; NASA/JPL-Caltech/MSSS;** *page 25*: **NASA/JPL/Space Science Institute;** *page 26*: **NASA/JPL-Caltech/SSI/PSI;** *page 27*: **Patricia.fidi.**

Chapter 3 A Quick Tour of the Universe
Page 32: **NASA/JPL/Space Science Institute; iStock.com/dottedhippo;** *page 34*: **iStock.com/CSA-Printstock;** *page 35*: **NASA/JPL/Space Science Institute; iStock.com/dottedhippo;** *page 37*: **ESA/Hubble, NASA, M. Kornmesser;** *page 38*: **NASA / Tim Pyle;** *page 39*: **iStock.com/exdez;** *page 41*: **Bruno Gilli/ESO** (http://www.eso.org/public/images/milkyway/) ; *page 42*: **The Hubble Heritage**

Team (AURA/STScI/NASA) NASA Headquarters - Greatest Images of NASA (NASA-HQ-GRIN); European Space Agency & NASA; NASA and The Hubble Heritage Team (STScI/AURA); Ray A. Lucas (STScI/AURA); NASA, ESA, and The Hubble Heritage Team STScI/AURA); *page 43*: **Adam Evans** (https://www.flickr.com/photos/8269775@N05) - licensed under the Creative Commons Attribution 2.0 Generic (https://creativecommons.org/licenses/by/2.0/deed.en) license; *page 44*: **iStock.com/Robotok**; *page 46*: **iStock.com/sadsadang**; **ESO** (http://www.eso.org/public/images/potw1304a/) - licensed under the Creative Commons Attribution 4.0 International (https://creativecommons.org/licenses/by/4.0/deed.en) license; *page 47*: **Richard Powell** (http://www.atlasoftheuniverse.com/nearsc.html) - licensed under the Creative Commons Attribution-Share Alike 2.5 Generic (https://creativecommons.org/licenses/by-sa/2.5/deed.en) license; *page 48*: **iStock.com/Magnilion**.

Chapter 4 The History of the Universe

Page 52: **Ian Beatty** (https://www.flickr.com/people/38719150@N00) from Amherst, MA, USA - licensed under the Creative Commons Attribution-Share Alike 2.0 Generic (https://creativecommons.org/licenses/by-sa/2.0/deed.en) license; **iStock.com/albertc111**; *page 53*: **iStock.com/PanosKarapanagiotis**; *page 55*: from **Edward Grant**, "Celestial Orbs in the Latin Middle Ages", Isis, Vol. 78, No. 2. (Jun., 1987); *page 57*: **iStock.com/ewg3D**; *page 58*: **Copernicus**, 1543; *page 59*: **iStock.com/wynnter**; *page 60*: **iStock.com/gameover 2012**; *page 62*: **iStock.com/TonyBaggett**; *page 63*: **NASA planetary photojournal**, (http://photojournal.jpl.nasa.gov/catalog/PIA00600); *page 64*: **iStock.com/traveler1116**; *page 66*; **iStock.com/quantum_orange**; *page 67*: **iStock.com/AlonzoDesign**; **iStock.com/Victor_85**; *page 68*: **iStock.com/AlonzoDesign**; **iStock.com/Victor_85**; **iStock.com/JdawnInk**; **iStock.com/bubaone**; *page 69*: **George J. Stodart**; *page 70*: **F. Schmutzer** (https://www.galerie-fach.de /index.php/en/schmutzer-f); **iStock.com/Noedelhap**; **iStock.com/Yevhenii Dubinko**; **iStock.com/Barbulat**; *page 72*: **Mysid** - licensed under the Creative Commons Attribution-Share Alike 3.0 Unported (https://creativecommons.org/licenses/by-sa/3.0/deed.en) license; **iStock.com/FluxFactory**; *page 74*: **Ruffnax** (Crew of STS-125)/NASA; *page 75*: **iStock.com/Yulia_Malinovskaya**; *page 76*: **NASA, ESA, and the Hubble Heritage Team (STScI/AURA)-ESA/Hubble Collaboration**; *page 77*: **iStock.com/bubaone**; *page 78*: **NASA Goddard Space Flight Center** (http://www.gsfc.nasa.gov/) under the guidance of the COBE Science Working Group (http://lambda.gsfc.nasa.gov/product /cobe/swg.cfm); **iStock.com/ttsz**; *page 80*: **NASA Goddard Space Flight Center** (http://www.gsfc.nasa.gov/) under the guidance of the COBE Science Working Group (http://lambda.gsfc.nasa.gov/product/cobe/swg.cfm); *page 81*: **NASA; ESA; G. Illingworth, D. Magee, and P. Oesch, University of California, Santa Cruz; R. Bouwens, Leiden University; and the HUDF09 Team**; *page 83*: **iStock.com/stphillips**; *page 85*: **iStock.com/t_kimura**; **iStock.com/Ale-ks**; *page 86*: **NASA, ESA and J. Hester (ASU)**; **iStock.com/exdez**; *page 87*: **iStock.com/Gunay Aliyeva**; **iStock.com/JdawnInk**; *page 88*: **NASA Goddard**.

Chapter 5 Life
Page 91: iStock.com/arakolog; *page 92*: NASA / Neil A. Armstrong; NASA; *page 94*: iStock.com/JuSun; iStock.com/mheim3011; *page 95*: iStock.com/wasant istock; iStock.com/ultramarinfoto; iStock.com/Freder; iStock.com/guenterguni; iStock.com/Denisapro; iStock.com/davidf; *page 96*: iStock.com/MR1805; *page 97*: Henry Maull and John Fox; iStock.com/cnythzl; *page 98*: iStock.com/GlobalP; *page 99*: iStock.com/Vac1; *page 100*: **Chiswick Chap** - licensed under the Creative Commons Attribution-Share Alike 2.5 Generic (https://creativecommons.org/licenses/by-sa/2.5/deed.en) license; *page 101*: **Martinowksy** – licensed under the Creative Commons Attribution-Share Alike 3.0 Unported (https://creativecommons.org/licenses/by-sa/3.0/deed.en) license; *page 102*: **David C. Marshall** - licensed under the Creative Commons Attribution-Share Alike 4.0 International (https://creativecommons.org/licenses/by-sa/ 4.0/deed.en) license; *page 103*: iStock.com/Wekwek; *page 104*: iStock.com/TefiM; *page 105*: iStock.com/JuSun; *page 106*: iStock.com/arakolog; *page 107*: iStock.com/ spawns; *page 108*: **Zephyris** - licensed under the Creative Commons Attribution-Share Alike 3.0 Unported (https://creativecommons.org/licenses/by-sa/3.0/ deed.en) license; *page 109*: **Universal Studios**; *page 110*: iStock.com/boschetto photography; iStock.com/Frederik Christoffersen; *page 111*: **Adenosine** - licensed under the Creative Commons Attribution-Share Alike 3.0 Unported (https://creativecommons.org/licenses/by-sa/3.0/deed.en) license; *page 112*: **Carny** - licensed under the Creative Commons Attribution 2.5 Generic (https://creativecommons.org/licenses/by/2.5/deed.en) license; *page 113*: **Oceanic and Atmospheric Administration** (http://oceanexplorer.noaa.gov/explorations/ 07fire/logs/hires/brothers_blacksmoker_hires.jpgNational; *page 114*: iStock.com/ MarcelC; *page 115*: **Goldstein lab** - tardigrades (https://www. flickr.com/photos/11562437@N03) - licensed under the Creative Commons Attribution Share Alike 2.0 Generic (https://creativecommons.org/licenses/by-sa/2.0/deed.en) license; **Schokraie E, Warnken U, Hotz-Wagenblatt A, Grohme MA, Hengherr S, et al.** (2012) - licensed under the Creative Commons Attribution 2.5 Generic (https://creativecommons.org/licenses/by/2.5/deed.en) license; PeterSnow; *page 117*: iStock.com/ChrisGorgio; iStock.com/Harald Schmidt; *page 118*: NASA/JPL/DLR; *page 119*: **NASA/JPL/Space Science Institute**; *page 120*: iStock.com/keiichihiki; *page 121*: **PublicDomainPictures** - made available under the Creative Commons CC0 1.0 Universal Public Domain Dedication (https://creativecommons.org/publicdomain/zero/1.0/deed.en); *page 123*: iStock.com/Impalastock; *page 124*: iStock.com/cisale; iStock.com/Artis777; *page 125*: **PublicDomainPictures** - made available under the Creative Commons CC0 1.0 Universal Public Domain Dedication (https://creativecommons. org/publicdomain/zero/1.0/deed.en); **Zephyris** - licensed under the Creative Commons Attribution-Share Alike 3.0 Unported (https://creativecommons. org/licenses/by-sa/3.0/deed.en) license; **iStock.com/spawns; Niall_Majury; FunkMonk (Michael B. H.)** - licensed under the Creative Commons Attribution-Share Alike 3.0 Unported (https:// creativecommons.org/licenses/by-sa/ 3.0/deed.en) license; iStock.com/buccaneership; iStock.com/d-l-b; iStock.com/

Dshnrgc; iStock.com/A-R-T-U-R; *page 127*: iStock.com/chinaface; *page 128*: iStock.com/skynesher; *page 129*: iStock.com/altmodern; *page 131*: iStock.com/DutchScenery; iStock.com/mbaysan; iStock.com/akiyoko; iStock.com/lappes; *page 132*: iStock.com/mocoo; *page 133*: iStock.com/cosmin4000; iStock.com/ Warpaintcobra; iStock.com/scibak; *page 135*: iStock.com/piola666; iStock.com/ AndreyPopov; iStock.com/ TheSP4N1SH; iStock.com/DJEPhotography; *page 136*: iStock.com/Ailime; *page 137*: iStock.com/Nataniil; *page 138*: iStock.com/ Nerthuz; *page 139*: iStock.com/AlonzoDesign.

Chapter 6 Wrong Place, Wrong Time

Page 140: iStock.com/MarinaMM; *page 141*: iStock.com/Anar Babayev; *page 142*: iStock.com/FreeSoulProduction; *page 143*: iStock.com/Daniela Mangiuca; *page 144*: iStock.com/AlonzoDesign; *page 145*: ALMA (ESO/NAOJ/NRAO), NASA/ESA Hubble Space Telescope, W. Zheng (JHU), M. Postman (STScI), the CLASH Team, Hashimoto et al.; *page 146*: ALMA (ESO/NAOJ/NRAO), NASA/ESA Hubble Space Telescope, W. Zheng (JHU), M. Postman (STScI), the CLASH Team, Hashimoto et al.; NASA, ESA and J. Hester (ASU); *page 147*: iStock.com/Pitris; *page 148*: iStock.com/Inchendio; *page 149*: iStock.com/ Matjaz Slanic; *page 150*: iStock.com/Natalia_80; *page 151*: NASA; ESA; G. Illingworth, D. Magee, and P. Oesch, University of California, Santa Cruz; R. Bouwens, Leiden University; and the HUDF09 Team; *page 152*: iStock.com/IkonStudio; *page 153*: NASA/Johns Hopkins APL/Steve Gribben; *page 154*: iStock.com/Anastasiia-Ku; *page 155*: NASA/JPL; *page 156*: iStock.com/gremlin; *page 157*: iStock.com/katrink03; iStock.com/Kenshi991; *page 158*: iStock.com/jameslee1; *page 159*: **ESA/Hubble & NASA** - released by the ESA under the Creative Commons Attribution 4.0 Unported license https://creativecommons.org/licenses/by/4.0/); *page 160*: **iStock.com/Kenshi991**; iStock.com/bubaone; iStock.com/Alex Belomlinsky; *page 161*: iStock.com/Alex Belomlinsky; iStock.com/Barbulat; iStock.com/Perception7; iStock.com/ janrysavy; *page 162*: iStock.com/alashi; *page 163*: iStock.com/VladT; *page 164*: iStock.com/Kenshi991; iStock.com/bubaone; iStock.com/Alex Belomlinsky; iStock.com/Diane Labombarbe; iStock.com/m-imagephotography; *page 165*: iStock.com/Alex Belomlinsky; iStock.com/Barbulat; iStock.com/Perception7; iStock.com/janrysavy; iStock.com/Diane Labombarbe; iStock.com/Andrii Shelenkov; *page 166*: **Mysid** - licensed under the Creative Commons Attribution-Share Alike 3.0 Unported (https://creativecommons.org/licenses/by-sa/3.0/deed.en) license; *page 167*: **iStock.com/Stockernumber2**; *page 168*: **Les Bossinas (Cortez III Service Corp.)/NASA.**

Chapter 7 Looking for Aliens

Page 170: iStock.com/Anthonycz; iStock.com/grebeshkovmaxim; *page 171*: iStock.com/dszc; *page 172*: **Roger W Haworth** (https://www.flickr.com/photos/rhaworth/) - licensed under the Creative Commons Attribution-Share Alike 2.0

Generic (https://creativecommons.org/licenses/by-sa/2.0/deed.en) license; *page 173*: **NASA/CXC/SAO (X-Ray); NASA/ JPL-Caltech (Infrared);** *page 174*: **Big Ear Radio Observatory and North American AstroPhysical Observatory (NAAPO); Jstuby at English Wikipedia** - licensed under the Creative Commons Attribution-Share Alike 3.0 Unported (https://creative commons.org/licenses/by-sa/3.0/deed.en) license; *page 175*: **NASA;** *page 176*: **Gregory R Todd** - licensed under the Creative Commons Attribution-Share Alike 3.0 Unported (https://creativecommons.org/licenses/by-sa/3.0/deed.en) license; *page 177*: **NASA/JPL; iStock.com/zirconicusso;** *page 178*: **NASA/JPL; iStock.com/BeingNothing; iStock.com/andymo; iStock.com/Iuliia Kanivets;** *page 179*: **NASA/JPL;** *page 180*: **iStock.com/bestdesigns;** *page 181*: **iStock.com/Dedy Setyawan; iStock.com/Avector; Amalex5** - licensed under the Creative Commons Attribution-Share Alike 4.0 International (https://creativecommons.org/licenses/by-sa/4.0/deed.en) license; *page 182*: **Bruno Gilli/ESO** (http://www.eso.org/public/images/ milky way/); **iStock.com/manopjk;** *page 183*: **Bruno Gilli/ESO** (http://www.eso.org/public/images/milkyway/); *page 184*: **iStock.com/artstorm;** *page 185*: **Bruno Gilli/ESO** (http://www.eso.org/public/images/milkyway/); *page 186*: **iStock.com/magnez2; iStock.com/Avector; iStock.com/dottedhippo;** *page 187*: **iStock.com/4x6;** *page 188*: **iStock.com/KatikaM; iStock.com/Anar Babayev; iStock.com/abluecup;** *page 191*: **iStock.com/Wdnet; iStock.com/diegograndi; Goran teken** - licensed under the Creative Commons Attribution-Share Alike 4.0 International (https://creativecommons.org/licenses/by-sa/ 4.0/deed.en) license; *page 192*: **iStock.com/Vac1;** *page 193*: **NASA; Sebastiano del Piombo;** *page 194*: **iStock.com/gremlin.**

Chapter 8 Have We Got It All Wrong?

Page 197: iStock.com/bubaone; *page 198*: iStock.com/grmarc; *page 199*: iStock.com/scanrail; iStock.com/Henrik5000; iStock.com/svedoliver; *page 200*: iStock.com/ChrisGorgio; *page 201*: iStock.com/thomasmales; iStock.com/twinsterphoto; iStock.com/Inchendio; iStock.com/bestdesigns; *page 202*: iStock.com/Chesky_W; *page 203*: NASA/JPL-Caltech; *page 204*: iStock.com/Irina_Qiwi; iStock.com/koya79; iStock.com/CSA Images; *page 205*: iStock.com/Diverstudio; *page 206*: iStock.com/AlonzoDesign; *page 207*: iStock.com/bubaone; iStock.com/sabuhinovruzov; NASA/JPL-Caltech/MSSS; *page 208*: iStock.com/olga_d; *page 209*: iStock.com/pialhovik; Orren Jack Turner, Princeton, NJ; *page 210*: iStock.com/Adobest; Kilo-Degree Survey Collaboration/H. Hildebrandt & B. Giblin/ESO - licensed under the Creative Commons Attribution 4.0 International (https://creativecommons.org/licenses/by/ 4.0/deed.en) license; *page 212*: iStock.com/pixelparticle; *page 213*: iStock.com/Yulia_Malinovskaya; *page 214*: Transocean Berlin; *page 215*: iStock.com/Pavel_R; *page 216*: iStock.com/DmitriyBurlakov; *page 217*: iStock.com/sakkmesterke; *page 218*: iStock.com/filo.

passim icons: iStock.com/bubaone; iStock.com/briang77; iStock.com/sjhaytov; iStock.com/Robotok; iStock.com/bamlou; iStock.com/quantum_orange; iStock.com/serkorkin; iStock.com/calvindexter.

Every effort has been made to trace all copyright holders and to obtain their permission for the use of copyright material. The publisher apologises for any errors or omissions in the above list and would be grateful if notified of any corrections that should be incorporated in future reprints or editions of this book.

248

About the Author

Stephen Rickard is an author and publisher with a particular interest in telling everybody about the wonder-full world we live in. He has written over 150 books and interactive titles for children and young adults, and is convinced that children aren't as daft as most adults seem to think.

His interactive multimedia title 'The History of the Universe' won the International Association for Media and Science award and was a finalist in the international EMMA awards.

He lives in Winchester in the south of England and no, he hasn't seen any aliens either.